DAVID CONSTANTINE

SELECTED POEMS

To

June '99.

John,

Many thanks for an inspiring week at Tŷ Newydd. Mike

Hannah Robuas

Lizzie Merrien

Steve W.

Sarah Series

Chris Griffiths

Matthew Morgans

SAM
☺ RJSH
x

Teresa Marsay

Guy Ramos

Oliver Rowney

Tom Hardy

dln Bord

Andrew Isley

Andrew Clark

Bill King

Paul Davies

THE CHASE HIGH SCHOOL, MALVERN

SELECTED POEMS

David Constantine

BLOODAXE BOOKS

First published 1991 by
Bloodaxe Books Ltd,
P.O. Box 1SN,
Newcastle upon Tyne NE99 1SN.

Bloodaxe Books Ltd acknowledges
the financial assistance of Northern Arts.

Cover reproduction by V & H Reprographics, Newcastle upon Tyne.

Cover printing by Index Print, Newcastle upon Tyne.

Printed in Great Britain by
Bell & Bain Limited, Glasgow, Scotland.

For Graham Sandiford

Acknowledgements

This book includes poems selected from David Constantine's previous collections, *A Brightness to Cast Shadows* (1980), *Watching for Dolphins* (1983) and *Madder* (1987), all published by Bloodaxe Books. His *Talitha Cumi* sequence first appeared in Noel Connor's poet-artist collaboration *Talitha Cumi* (Bloodaxe Books, 1983), a response by artists and poets to the story of Jairus's daughter, the young girl whom Jesus raised from the dead with the words '*Talitha cumi*' – or, 'Little girl, awake.' *Mappa Mundi* was first published by the Five Seasons Press in 1984.

Acknowledgements are due to the editors of the following publications in which some of the new poems in the fourth section of this book were first published: *Cambridge Review, First and Always* (Faber, 1989), *Orbis, Poetry Book Society Anthologies* (PBS/Hutchinson, 1989, 1990, 1991), *PN Review, Poetry Review, Quarry, Rhinoceros, The Rialto, Smoke,* and *Verse.* 'Jailed for Life' was broadcast on *Poetry Now* (BBC Radio 3). 'Mandeville', 'The Forest', 'I should not be dreaming of you like this', 'Local Historian', 'Clare leaves High Beach', 'Under that bag of soot', 'He arrived, towing a crowd' and 'In the ocean room' were broadcast on *The Living Poet* (BBC Radio 3).

The cover shows a detail from *The Battle of the Lapiths and the Centaurs* by Piero di Cosimo, reproduced by courtesy of the Trustees, the National Gallery, London.

Contents

NEW POEMS

FROM **A BRIGHTNESS
TO CAST SHADOWS**

(1980)

'As our bloods separate'

As our bloods separate the clock resumes,
I hear the wind again as our hearts quieten.
We were a ring: the clock ticked round us
For that time and the wind was deflected.

The clock pecks everything to the bone.
The wind enters through the broken eyes
Of houses and through their wide mouths
And scatters the ashes from the hearth.

Sleep. Do not let go my hand.

Birdsong

Most are sleeping, some
Have waited hopelessly for mercy,
Others even by this will not be stayed.
But we who have not slept for quantity
Of happiness have heard
The dawn precipitate in song
Like dewfall.

We think our common road a choir of trees.

'Daffodils in vases'

Daffodils in vases, watch them daily
For the first touch of dying, even
The blossom you came carrying
Of cherry and almond I will raise
The fire with tonight to see
You naked by, only the tulips
Wider and wider leave them opening
Until their petals fall
In gouts on the marble hearth.

'But most you are like'

But most you are like
The helpless singing of birds
To whom the light happens
On whom it falls
And at whose purity of voice
The skies weep and there is a pause
In all the world before beginning
And before the ending.

A Brightness to Cast Shadows

And now among them these dark mornings yours
Ascendant and of a brightness to cast shadows.
Love the winter, fear
The earlier and earlier coming of the light
When in the mantle blue we turn our dead faces.

The Fool

Be still, only believe me, said the Fool
Love and with impartial pleasure
Touched her breasts and mine

Ignoring any history of lovers and children
But as a matter of sole beauty
Admired their present marks

On my breasts now and see, he said,
The lighter halo of hers. A while,
The dancers' above earth,

We did take hands she and I
And the Fool in a ring against
Outliving Time

Whom I saw sardonically looking
To enter the round between us
Facing the boy Love.

'Eyes wide with the moon'

Eyes wide with the moon
He speaks in a tangle of words
How cold her hair was

He would have me imagine the moon
The briars the bedded leaves
A place out of the cold

The cold shines into me
The bright face takes my breath
Withers my warm reply

He will have warmed her hands
A tree he says the branches her cold hair
Among the embracing roots

She will have been drawn into
The moon in his eyes her tongue
Into his mouth...

'You are distant, you are already leaving'

You are distant, you are already leaving
You will have seemed here only between trains
And we are met here in the time of waiting
And what you last want is our eyes on you.

We shall have said nothing, we shall have done
Nothing in all that meantime there will
Have been not one gift pleasing us
You will have looked away and only behind
The pane of glass taking your seat with strangers
Being conveyed from here and when there is
No stay of parting you will smile perhaps
And give your face then the small mercy of weeping.

'In the meantime, in the waiting time'

In the meantime, in the waiting time
There is no present stay, we are
Not capable of interlude, we seem
In talk attending to elsewhere
And that it wants a while yet to the sun's going
Will not warm us in the long shade of our own.
Giving nothing to time present how
We overburden time remaining

With what we have not said we know
And raise the burden to impossible. Remembering
How cold under this future promontory
We studied only to effect evasions
Love do not elsewhere think of death as mountains
Shutting out the sun even before midday.

Eurydice

He turned. Nor was she following. The god
Shrugged and departed – on such a fool's errand
He will in future be harder to engage.

She remained staring into the black pool
Transfixed
As though in love but without
Any pleasure in the beloved face.

Soon there were none among the living
Who could remember her
As living. For her recovery
She imagined one who should descend the interminable spirals
Never having seen her live and yet
Imagining she might, one who would climb
Confident of the daylight and of her following.

On the coming of such a one
She waited. And not
At a crossroads but
In Hell.

The Damned

I see the damned are like this:
Loquacious to no effect, for ever
Coming to the end of their poor abilities,
Words failing them, neither

Their blows nor their embraces
Serving them better,
Incapable of nakedness
They rasp their hands on one another

Like two dead trees' branches
They sound the skull with a long finger,
Their speech is a sort of trepanning, lidless
The eyes watch barrenly for ever.

Dawn: slow fall of song...The sky
I imagine white, streaming with mercy.

'All wraiths in Hell are single'

All wraiths in Hell are single though they keep
Company together and go in troops like sheep.
None meets a lover from the former world,
No souls go hand in hand, round each is curled
The river Acheron. They suffer most
Who violently joined the myriad host,
Who angrily to spite love in the face
Before their time intruded on that place,
Putting themselves by pride beyond recovery,
Beyond sight, beyond calling. They seem to be
Alive among the dead wishing the thing undone
By which they put themselves beyond Acheron.
Divested of anger, cold, without reprieve
Sine die along the riverbanks they grieve.
They hear one calling after love into the black
But cannot answer and cannot come back.

Streams

It was never enough only to trace their courses
Nor to follow alongside, and the best were pathless,
But I must be always in them straddling the waters,
Clawing among roots, fingers poked in the wet moss
And parting the long grasses for a grip of stone.
Best to be naked as well as possible to feel
The switch of birches, smooth trunks of rowan,
Sticks and fronds of fern and tassels of hazel.

Hand on either bank and foothold to embrace
The reclining falls and rainbowed round to sunder
The water like a tree for a breathless space...
And for the smell of mud there is in worming under
The grasses, the toppled boles are finger-soft
And the glimmering rock flakes like the bark of birches.
The eyes may be shut with moss in some such cleft,
Mouth and nose pressed to in a deep kiss.

One I remember climbing from the blue renowned
As deepest of all the lakes and verdant black
Among lawns and pines the enclosed garden ground
To where, between scented equal hills, my back
And praising arms brightly arrayed in sun,
Wet-lipped from a hoof of sedge the water grew.
You will have thought below I'd gone for heaven
When I stood there at the sky on the brink of all blue.

Lamb

A lamb lay under the thorn, the black
Thorn bending by the last broken wall
And grasping what it can.

The dead lamb picketed a ewe.
She cropped round, bleating

And chewing in that machinal way of sheep.
And although she backed to a safe distance,
When I climbed down towards her lamb
Through a gap in the wall,
It was as if painfully paying out the fastening cord.

The crow was there, also
At a safe distance, waiting for the ewe to finish;
And sidled off a further yard or so,
Waiting until I too should have finished.

In high relief the lamb
Lay leaping, the small hooves down-pointed at
The instant of spring, one foreleg already flexing
To step forward on the air.
The head like a new tennis ball,
But stained; the mouth grim as a shark's.
For the eye had gone, and all
That swelled from the socket was a black bubble.

The ewe, chewing and mourning, and
The crow, that fathoms the convenient eye-hole,
Had approached on either hand. The bubble burst
And a hole sank such a depth into the skull
That not a sound returned.

I backed away, and again
The ewe could circle the navel of her earth;
But the crow, with a hunching of wings and a jump sideways,
Glanced over the raised cloak of one wing,
And trod, and grasped its feet into the ground,
And could wait
Until hunger stretched and parted
The cord, and the monotony
Of chewing deadened any pain.

Even from river level I knew the place,
In the angle where the wall descends,
And I thought I could make out the bush,
And the white dot of the dead lamb under it.

And I thought in that place there is always an exit
From the light of the sun, an issue of darkness
Opened by the crow's black beak. I know the way,
Into the hillside,
Through the eye of a lamb.

That was in April, when
Snow still lies beyond the wall, before
The blackthorn flowers.

Near Zennor

Coming among the grazing boulders
They herded them into hedges
And tended their own cattle on the vacated ground.

They made houses of the stones skirting the carn
And beyond mounds for their dead
In a quiet herd, and paths from place to place.

It is not easy now to distinguish between
Their circles and the collars of the dead mines.
The hedges and paths are as they were.

And a stone riven by frost from the mother flank
Their feet have gone over across water,
Their heads bowed under daily into the house.

To go back unobtrusively under the moor
Is one grace of austerity, to flower
And be quarried for a successor's building.

The Lane

The lane's especial beauty, why especially
You are at home there, is the way it has
Of winding unhurriedly and for no remembered reason,
And this I have come to love more even than
The scent and the quiet between its hedges.

Even alone now, though by nature one
For landmarks on the horizon to be reached by dark,
As far as is possible I adopt your way
And walk in the lane's good time that never offers
More to our view than we should be content with;

And after the farm becomes impassable,
Under the vaulting of both hedges' trees,
In any season but of the hardest drought or frost:
Which ultimatum at the outset lends
Your dawdling its complacency.

For these your and the lane's own qualities
And that in special once, a moonless night
And close with honeysuckle,
The sea pausing between wave and wave,
You came to meet me down it,

Nowhere is more home. A certainty
Of love is that of taking hands
And elsewhere turning into this same lane,
Sending ahead the old precursors:
The fox, the cat, the finches.

Journey

Leaving the watered villages
The ash and poplar cool in their appearances
We came the companionable stream and I
To the last farm by and by.

For the whitethorn there
That was in flower later than anywhere
The girl water would not continue with me
I left her under the last tree.

Then some days following
I cast the long shadows of morning and evening
At noon I rode the sun on my shoulder
I was without water.

The white sheep lay
Like the remaining snow in February
On the north side of walls, in holes they hid
In poor embraces of shade.

Beyond pasture, beyond enclosure
On the common land of rock how far below were
Any cwm, any cradled pool and the water-veined
Wide folds. There intervened

No cloud, no bough between
Myself and the sun, only a hawk was shone
Steadily upon me in the grip of noon
I trod my shadow down.

I dreamed of the girl Artemis
She wore the ash and the poplar in a green dress
She led three burning hounds and seeing me
She smiled and set them free.

'Pitiless wind'

Pitiless wind, the hedges
Queue for dole, there is
No warmth in line. More
Pitiless light, searching
From under snowclouds, level

Like the wind, discovering
Rags, cans and what
Have been hugged to the heart
Since May: nests, all
Empty but one or two

And these, harboured since there
Were leaves, containing small
Frail skeletons bent
Like embryos. The wind, the light
Show up our few belongings.

'The wind has bared the stars'

The wind has bared the stars,
The skeletons, the after-images.

The life of trees has flown,
Their swarm of leaves, their hail of birds, their bone-

Dry sticks tap-tap,
Their blades slant in the earth's cold lap,

And leafless we are shown
To be rooted apart, two trees not one.

The dust and hail belong
Nowhere particular, our leaves and song;

Disperse among the stars,
Our skeletons, our after-images.

'Trewernick'

1

House in the marsh, it was always at evening
    We saw you first, over reed-tops, through a haze
Of lichened willows, after twelve hours travelling.
    Beyond our terminus the daylight set
Slowly from off the remaining terra firma,
    But we retraced our passage through the reeds
To the gate and threshold among apple trees before
    The night came roosting in your cypresses.
House in the marsh, had you taught your children nothing
    But the reliable grace of such a welcome
Yet you had charged a family for generations
    So that they shone with the warm glow of gold.

2

Mounding the earth, facing it in with rusty stone,
    Raising upon the borders of culture
Fine distinctions in heather and broom gently you made
    Your garden join the field, your tended plants
Confused their colours with a savage hedge behind
    Of gorse and bramble. Had I to indicate
Your tact with rooted lives I'd put my finger on
    That sewing of your garden to the fields
Which rise then stitched with hedges in a mild gradient
    To Ludgvan Church and culminate on ground
Of granite where the brow is wreathed with defences
    And the threadbare back pockmarked with tumuli.

3

One year the marvel was a bush vermilion
    With lucent fruit, one bush, glowing like Mars,
Kept at its brilliant prime for us to see. There followed
    By our hands the abundant bleeding of the tree,
The million berries mounded in a basket. Your
    Own skill is that of transferring the garden
Into the recesses of the house, of cupping
    The summer in a household hoard with no

Diminishing of warmth or light. In jars on shelves
  In cupboards stood the store of amber, garnet,
Jade and when the year closed down the house glowed at its core
  With the essences your working hands put by.

4

Dear ones in Cornwall how golden and leisurely
  The light stays. Nobody can be in haste
Not even to ask for or dispose of stories,
  But a shyness which is perhaps the sun
Slanting so low causes companions to hide their eyes
  And soonest to fall silent, admiring
The growth of a tree set at a birth ten years ago.
  Then to seek anything would seem discourteous
In the fullness we can almost hold to be lasting.
  Again we shall leave and you will write to us
How in October the sky blackened with starlings
  And fell on that mock cornfield like a pall.

5

But now the children are handing you down apples
  That will sweeten the dark under the roof
Another winter. Then the reeds, under a cold sky,
  Are warm-coloured like corn and fire by fire
Towards another spring you burn the logs of cypress
  And apple wood. How much is into us
Of all your gifts and through the long attenuation
  Shall we be able to keep hold? Think the hands
We see on tombs are clasped not only in farewell
  But to impart and thereby are we bound.
By touch the generations glow. If not reunion
  Those held hands are at least continuance.

'Suddenly she is radiant again'

Suddenly she is radiant again.
She sees rainbows through her wet lashes;
In the brilliant light her wet cheeks glisten;
Her talk resumes like a brook, as fast and careless.

She has to suffer the interruption
Of sobs still, that have the bad manners
To arrive after the thunder has already gone
Over the hill, insisting they are hers.

We were a black sky only a minute ago,
Now I'm the one cloud in her clear heaven.
I haven't even begun yet to undo
The hideous knot of anger she tied me in.

I'm like a black old lump of winter snow
Bitterly facing the spring sun. Fair
Is always fair and the ugly, be they ever so
Much in the right, are not welcome anywhere.

I'm not a stone, I'm dirty snow that in
Her sunlight melts. It has no choice but to.
Soon I begin to feel I've been forgiven:
I go down on my knees and fasten her shoe.

'For years now'

For years now through your face the skull has shown
Nearer than through their living surface
The hills' bulk of dead stone;

And for years, watching you sleeping in that chair,
I have wished you might die with your face and hands composed,
Quietly sleeping there,

And trusted death to be so easy on you
That now one moment you would be sleeping and now
Have ceased without seeming to.

But today, watching you dead, I cannot think that there
Is any such slow passing into death from life
That the one might seem the other.

Finally the gap is absolute. Living
At all you were never nearly dead
And dead there is nothing

Vital of you in the abandoned face.
But the lack, the difference, has such nearness
We could almost embrace.

Waiting

We have gathered together
The things you will need immediately
And set them on a table
By the bed you will be born in.
You have three drawers to your name
Of clothes for the first months.

I go from room to room. The house
Is waiting. Our hands are ready.
Even not yet knowing you
We love you; grateful
For how you have increased us; glad
We have it in us to put out new love.

Hands

Round my finger, like a bird perching...
In my hollow palm, like a pebble, a cool bud...
Idling with his hands.

O hands...

The interslotting of our fingers and beckoning in
Your palm and tonguing of
The skin that tautens between thumb and index...
Your hand gives him the breast and the ring shines.

How cold her hands were latterly, and visible
The painful jointings of the long bones.
The firelight shone almost through and the blood's
Network with its many nodes and bruises
Was shown like that of a leaf.
She lagged her ring with cotton but
The days loosened it again.

His sharp nails are like
The fragments of rosy shell lying in pools.

O sands, o future rocks...

In Memoriam 8571 Private J.W. Gleave
who was at Montauban, Trônes Wood and Guillemont

'So many without memento...'

1. *Prologue: The Children*

I bade them climb: they must have come to the very crest
And it was beautiful to see them shine
Not steadily but charged at a sudden moment
And for only such duration as the light allowed
The light they caught upon their faces from the face
Already we should have thought sunk out of sight.

There are some dead we see and even see by;
They glimmer for a generation, our looking
Lends them more luminance. I saw the father,
Whom no one can rekindle, appear to shine
Over the earth in the eyes of the gazing children.
They cast his face upon my white paper.

2. *After how many Novembers...*

How soon, I wonder, after how many Novembers
   Did the years begin to seem not paces
Interminably around a pit nor steps deserting
   A place, but slow degrees by which she came
Over the curve of the world into that hemisphere
   His face rose in? Again we have given ground,
The dark advances an hour into the afternoon,
   In the interlude between cloud and horizon
A mild sun scythes the field – so by the last winter
   After an illness and before her death
We saw a similar light dawn on the woman
   Who had been a widow more than fifty years.

She lingered in the doorway of the living-room
  Impelled as people leaving are to say
Some word more than goodnight. I have seen her eyes shining
  Bright as a young girl's on that threshold
Bright with tears. She found nothing to say. But having
  Her purse in hand the purse she had kept house from
For generations since the Queen died she took out
  The new, neat, folded notes of her pension
And to the children and their children and their child
  Disposed of these. We do not like to watch
A person look for words nor by whatever gestures
  Taking her leave of table, hearth and chair.

She went to her own room where everything was ready
  To leave, the furniture of her married life
Though in another house, one he had never seen.
  But in that mirror he had seen his face,
They will have stood side by side and looked at themselves
  She will have stood by herself and remembered.
And always she held the two or three photographs
  Which light had fallen on man and wife to make
In an envelope with the notice of his death
  As if to cross over with these in hand
That she should know him again who had been effaced
  And he should know her who had lived and aged.

3. *Notification*

It was the painful duty of Lieutenant Thomas Dinsdale
On Army Form B 104-82
In an envelope the postwoman shrank from touching
To notify my grandmother of her altered state.
The women stood by, they followed the post like crows:
To whom would such a communication come
That morning, to what woman by the hand of a woman
Whose job it was daily to visit that village of streets
And lay the stigmata on certain doors?

So the news came from Guillemont to Salford 5
After a lapse of weeks during which time
She had known no better than to believe herself a wife.

4. *By word of mouth*

Not having seen him die and when
Upon their notification nothing followed
Neither the body to her hearth
Nor any of the late soldier's effects
A little while
As though the outcome could be put in doubt
She trimmed her mourning with a thread of hope
She kept the Suitor from her husband's chair
Showed Death the door
Nightly, until the evenings were long.
He called then with a companion from France.
The neighbours, who miss nothing, saw
Only the soldier leave.

5. *Récit*

No messenger in the tragedies
So mean but coming to the wife, the mother
Or any beloved woman waiting
Recounts fittingly the dead man's death
In alexandrines or iambics
And honours him in the telling.
But who the pal was is not remembered
Nor what he said, nor what the questions were
She had the heart to put nor whether
She lamented there and then, praising the qualities
Of the man lost and hiding her face as queens do
In her apron. Not a word, not the place itself
Reached me in his pronunciation
But as to how and where
She only shrugged her shoulders
And perhaps she had that from the messenger
Who did not tell her that the night was very short
And began in a barrage of phosgene gas
And ended in a thick fog
And a barrage of high explosive
As they moved around the southern edge of Trônes Wood
Across seven hundred yards of open ground
Gently sloping to the village of Guillemont

In an attack understood to be hopeless
But serving the French on their right
Whose attack was also hopeless
And that somewhere before the wire
He was obliterated
In gas and night and fog.

6.

But by November the congregation of widows
    Being told it was a reasonable sacrifice
Their men had made saw mutilated trees bedecked
    With bloody tatters and being nonetheless
Promised a resurrection of the body
    They saw God making their men anew out of
The very clay. These women having heard from soldiers
    However little from the battlefield
Towards All Saints gathered black gouts from the elder
    Among their children stared at the holy tree
And envied Christ his hurts fit to appear in.
    Some then insisted on a photograph
Taken before the harm was done – which face they caused
    To appear in the hideous crater of their lives
Upon its slimy water. In time while she pursued
    With wrung hands her business as a widow
The water cleared. On the surface of a peaceful pool
    Decently framed the face shone steadily.

7.

There being no grave, there being not even one
Ranked among millions somewhere in France,
Her grief went without where to lay its head.
She would have rested sooner had she had
Or had she even learned somewhere there was
A well-kept place where he was lying dead.

She could not even think him out of harm:
He must be hurt somewhere by every shell,
Somewhere his mouth could not get breath for gas.
She would have scavenged all his body home
Into the shelter of if not her house
At least the roofed and hidden well-walled grave.

But of what comfort is the body home
Which here or there cannot embrace or smile?
And of what comfort is the body whole?
Only the rich and saints do not corrupt.
She almost thought there were degrees of death
And he was more dead piecemeal and abroad.

There being nowhere but the family grave
She went and called her grief out of the air
And coaxed it to alight upon the stone
That did not bear his name. Upon that absence
She grieved as though it were the greater one
And death was lured almost within her view.

She set that feature on the featureless
Visibly everlasting plain of death
She trod a path, she made some little inroad
And placing three or four remembrance days
She netted in their few interstices
Glimpses that she could bear out of the deep.

8. *Roll of Honour*

She never saw his name at Thiepval
Nor even in Manchester Cathedral
But on Liverpool Street outside the Mission Hall
There was a Roll of Honour on the wall

Affixed in nineteen-seventeen
And this she will have seen
Daily (until the Blitz
Blew all the names to bits).

The enlisted men – there were no officers –
Were columned street by street and hers
Was one of those already crossed. By rights
The Vicar should have come at nights

And crossed the others one by one
Until the toll was done.

9. *Like shrapnel*

Like shrapnel in the lucky ones
She carried fragments in her speech
Remarkable to grandchildren
But to herself accustomed
Like rise and shine and left
Left...he had a good home and he left
And a long, long trail a-winding...

Coltsfoot

Coming before my birthday they are forever your flowers
Who are dead and at whose hand
I picked them on the allotments and blitzed land.

Coltsfoot and Larches

I love coltsfoot that they
Make their appearance into life among dead grass:
Larches, that they
Die colourfully among sombre immortals.

Johnny

Faces, faces, says Johnny,
The perceptions lingering, lingering, in general
And in the home, for what
Does a man see on the dead wall of his life,
A jakes wall, but among the writing
Faces, faces, beating the brow against?

Jimmy

The belly: a big craw
Come out of the shirt like a goitre;
An angry cross of scars.

Jimmy, your face has the texture of fungus.
Your tears drop like fat
In rapid beads, from under the hair
The head is weeping,

They hit the table between your bloody knuckles.

Billy

The lines, Billy, I am thinking
I should like to run a finger down, they rive
Your face to the bone chin.

Your daughter, you are saying, said
The aborted one, Norma, 15, fuck off
Back to the asylum Dad, your own dad,
You are saying, home
From prison strung you to the mangle naked
And beat you to a jelly. I

Am thinking Billy when he weeps
It is the rent, the creases fill but
What about the rent? And more
Than ever I should like to put a finger in
The runnels of your face
That wants some beating for cadaverousness.

Stuart

Stuart, I would not begin at once
With the obvious. It seems
Too many have and she
Is none the warmer. Her beak
Would gnaw through bone.

The mouth, I grant you, is
A whiskerless rat's; raw
Her hands and one of those trees on the estate
The kids have stripped
Would be as abundant to embrace.

Under hers, as motherly as hail,
The child has lost his tongue. Where then
Should you begin? The eyes
Look for the worst. Could you only
Show them some goodwill.

'But with a history of ECT'

But with a history of ECT
And separation Milburn Margaret Mrs
Did not attain the obliterating sea
She got no further than the DHSS
And on a Friday in the public view
Lodged on the weir as logs do.

During the rush-hour she was attended to
And all the terraces of Gallowgate
Watched the recovery of this female who
Went in the river at the age of thirty-eight.
She did not pass unnoticed but instead
Got seen to being dead.

And at the inquest the Acting Coroner
Inquiring as to how and why she died
Exculpated both the hospital and her
Emeritus husband who identified
That frozen woman in the mortuary
He had four children by.

'Dennis Jubb is dead'

Dennis Jubb is dead. But considering
He certainly never went short of smokes
Nor a dreg of something in the morning
Not to mention the lovely picture books

He often sat behind his barrow in doorways
Grinning at the innocent passers-by over
And when you take into account that all these
Were extras to a living wage we do aver

That Mr Dennis Jubb did not do too bad
Bearing in mind as well all the other things he had
As for example he had a loving mate
And a revitalized house on the Fairhope Road Estate

And that he lived to be forty, a good age,
And got his death by burning on the front page.

'I suppose you know this isn't a merry-go-round'

I suppose you know this isn't a merry-go-round.
The man won't stop it when you think you've had your money's worth.
To get off at all you'll have to jump
And risk breaking your neck
And where you fall will appear strange
And not where you got on.

These have not been flat revolutions
On the enduring earth
But spirals down.
You are lower now.

That being so
I would almost advise you to stay put.
You are in the company of your friends
And for a change
You can always stagger from a horse to a white elephant.
Nobody seems to mind.

FROM **WATCHING
FOR DOLPHINS**
(1983)

Mary Magdalene and the Sun

Hugging her breasts, waiting in a hard garden
For Sun, the climber, to come over the hill,
Disconsolate, the whore Mary Magdalene,
She of the long hair. But Sun meanwhile,

Scaling inch by inch the steep other side,
At last got a grip with his fingers on the rim
And hoisted himself up. She saw the spikes of his head,
His brow, then his brazen face. So after his swim

Leander's fingers appeared on Hero's sill
And he hauled himself inside, naked and salt
And grinning. She closed her eyes and let him feel
Her open face, uncrossed her arms and felt

Him warm her breasts and throat. Thereupon a cock
Crowed once, very red. And something came and stood
Between her and the Sun, something cold, and 'Look,'
It moaned. And there, casting a shadow, naked

And bled white was the nailed man, he whose
Blessing arms they fixed on a beam, and he crouched
There gibbering of love and clutching his
Thin shoulders and begging to be touched.

He was encrusted above the eyes with black,
And maculed in the hands and feet and in his side,
And through clacking teeth he begged her to touch him, and 'Look,'
He moaned, 'at this and this that they did,'

Showing the holes. Sun, the joker, though,
Had leapfrogged him, and more cocks crowed,
And down the green hillside and through
The waking garden the waters of irrigation flowed

And plenteous happy birdsong from the air,
As Sun diminished the ghosts of fruit trees on the grass
And over the nailed man's shoulder stroked the harlot's hair
And fingered open the purple sheaths of crocuses.

Lazarus to Christ

You are forgetting, I was indeed dead
Not comatose, not sleeping, and could no more
Wish for resurrection than what we are before
Can wish for birth. I had already slid

Four days down when you hauled me back into the air.
Now they come to watch me break bread
And drink the wine, even the tactful plead
With dumb faces to be told something, and, dear,

Even you, who wept for me and of whom it is said
You know all things, what I mutter in nightmare
I believe you lie awake to overhear.
You too are curious, you too make me afraid

Of my own cold heart. However I wash
I cannot get the foist out of my flesh.

Christ to Lazarus

They faltered when we came there and I knew very well
They were already leaving me. Not one
Among your mourners had any stomach to go on,
And when they moved the stone and we could smell

Death in his lair they slid off me like cloud
And left me shining cold on the open grave
Crying for you and heaving until Death gave
And you were troubled in your mottled shroud.

They hid their eyes, they begged me let you stay,
But I was adamant, my friend. For soon
By a loving father fiercer than any moon
It will be done to me too, on the third day.

I hauled you out because I wanted to.
I never wept for anyone but you.

Minos, Daedalos and Pasiphaë

Minos himself, like any supplicant,
Came clumsily asking how it might be done.
Daedalos smiled: nothing the heart might want
Surprised him, who had Ikaros for a son.

None knew, so perfect was the counterfeit,
None among those who ran to take the bull,
Dropping bewildered from coition, in a net;
Only the King, who watched. The woman, full,

Penned what she bore in the Labyrinth to die.
It grew. They heard it roaring for the light of day,
They heard it blunder through the passages and try –
Sobbing with a human hope – another way.

They wished a slayer would come. Their normal child
Looked monstrous to the Queen. Daedalos smiled.

Priapics

1

Godling, your mother, the smiling Aphrodite, though she loved
    Nothing so much as cock, when she had born you to
Bacchus, hid her face, and neither would own you, seeing
    What had lain covert in the divine heart of each.
Associate of Pan, impossible to clothe, they hid you in greenery,
    In gardens to threaten thieves, or you stood where roads met,
Ambushing wayfarers with their desires, and, as Priapus of Harbours,
    To you poor sailors prayed, leaving their girls.

2

He threatened with his club impartially
    Thieves of either sex; served them alike
When, by the bed of leeks or the bed of thyme
    Caught trespassing, boy or girl turned tail.

3

Caught fig-stealing girls departed that garden
    Only on payment of an equitable fine.
'Figs for figs,' he demanded, and the luscious part
    Of girls, the cleft and honeyed, the conducive,
The petalled-back, must cap his club. Then he arranged
    Their stolen figs coolly in a nest of vine-leaves,
And showed them out of the garden by a secret door
    Where trespassers might enter when they liked.

4

Who are under the orbs and sceptre of King
    Prick when he says jump they jump for his
Slightest wish is their command throughout the hours of
    Daylight and darkness. Nowhere by that
Soft nose may you not lead them and to their hearts
    The way comes thence. Dead they will all
Push up the earth in molehills, the humblest
    Among them emerging as *phalli*
Impudici, while the best some flowery
    Hill will brandish as an Attis pine.

5

How soon evasive girls walking alone and wishing
    Always to bear thus deep under their surfaces
The shadows, the quiet clouds, the shaken moon; being
    No further in than glances, than the casting,
Like dew on webs, of first love on the common courtesies,
    Have halted at him set in his covert place,
Grinning, upreared, always too soon, a hamfist,
    Botching their dreams with sense so blunt and tearing.
'Leave oil,' he says, 'leave honey, you would be wise
    To smooth me. For I am at the root and how
You grow and flower in the light and how you fume in scent
    And pass from substance to vapour, crying for love,
Crying for the happiness of your rendered soul, derives
    From me.' Some women by the way they smile, some wives,
One knows they wear the root-god for an amulet and mirror
    Skies still and every fineness of sun and stars.

'Misshapen women'

Misshapen women on the Fairhope Road Estate when the wind
    Presses upon you hurrying to the meat factory
Your breasts are not discovered through a thin chiton, nor down
    The inguinal triangle do the lovely folds ripple;
And when the sun, winking behind the scrap heap, ends your days
    You cannot face it smiling like caryatids,
Whom only marble burdened, for you are not fit to be
    Regarded from any angle. Only from above,
To Infinite Mercy, are your unbuttonable forms and your
    Poor mouths not an eyesore, and in an interlude
When no sun plays and no sarcastic wind He may drizzle
    Some charity upon you from a grey heaven.

The Door

Yes, that is the door and behind it they live,
But not grossly as we do. Through a fine sieve
Their people pass the incoming air. They are said
To circulate thoughtfully in walled gardens, the aged –
And they live long – wheeling in chairs. They exchange
Nothing but traditional courtesies. Most strange
However is their manner of dying, for they know the hour,
When it comes, as old elephants do. They devour
Their usual breakfast of plovers' eggs and rise
Then or are lifted by the janitors and without goodbyes
They step or are borne aloft through that door there –
And thus they end. For of course meeting the air,
The air we breathe, they perish instantly,
They go all into dust, into dead dust, and Stanley,
The Sweeper, comes with his brush and shovel and little cart
And sweeps them up and shovels them not apart
But into one black plastic bag with dimps, dog-shit
And all our common dirt. But this they intend and it
Signals their gracious willingness to reside
In the poor heart of life, once they have died.

'Pity the drunks'

Pity the drunks in this late April snow.
They drank their hats and coats a week ago.
They touched the sun, they tapped the melting ground,
In public parks we saw them sitting round
The merry campfire of a cider jar
Upon a crocus cloth. Alas, some are
Already stiff in mortuaries who were
Seduced by Spring to go from here to there,
Putting their best foot forward on the road
To Walkden, Camberwell or Leeds. It snowed.
It met them waiting at the roundabout.
They had no hats and coats to keep it out.
They did a lap or two, they caught a cough.
They did another lap and shuffled off.

Boy finds tramp dead

But for your comfort, child, who found him curled
With crizzled cheeks, his hands in his own ice,
Among the trapped dead birds and scraps of girls,

His spectacles and broken teeth put by
Along the window with a pile of pence,
Remember this man was the son of nobody,

Father, brother, husband, lover, friend
Of nobody, and so by dying alone
With rats hurt nobody. Perhaps he joined

And mended easily with death between
Newspaper sheets in drink and did not wake
Too soon, at midnight, crying to sleep again,

Alive and hung on cold, beyond the embrace
Of morning, the warm-handed. He was pressed
Together when you found him, child, but names

Had left his lips of wicked men released
Quickly in sunlight and of one who baked
Asleep inside a kiln and many at rest

With cancer in the casual ward or knocked
Under fast wheels. These he conjured with
To Christ as instances of mercy, being racked

Himself on boards beside a prolapsed hearth.
His vermin died. The morning's broken glass
And brightening air could not pick up his breath.

Little by little everything in him froze,
Everything stopped: the blood in the heart's ways,
The spittle in his mouth, his tongue, his voice.

Elegy

We hear you spoken of as a dead man
And where you were there is new growth of obituaries.
Someone has met an eyewitness from Darlington –
A liar, it is true. We had thought this was
Only the interruption of one of your stories

And you were working slowly on a smoke
And, tilting your indoor trilby, would appear
Through clouds soon and would broach
Your silence waiting like an untouched beer
For a man back from the gents. Remember the bloke

So bent with *arthuritis* that for his wake
They tied him to a board and in the small hours
Some joker cut his cords and, with a creak,
He sat up grinning? In a digger's jaws
Rising in a shroud of snow at bitter daybreak

You cleared a building-site; the mortuary men,
Summoned to shift you, dewy, from the road,
Have brought their breakfasts up and dropped their load
When you opened an eye. Time and again
From under newspaper we fetched you in,

A foetal stiff. Around the cup you set
Your fingers like a broken basket
And thawing your nose in tea began to tell
The story of a man from Motherwell
Who swallowed three hundred goldfish for a bet

And lived. You lived the part: the Indian doctor
Offering to amputate; nice Ronnie Kray
Visiting his mam; Lord Londonderry
Addressing your father like the man next door.
You hooked yourself a stooge when necessary.

If the liar from Darlington was right then now
The devil is leaning on his fork and you
Are keeping him waiting while you toast your bum
And roll a smoke for what is still to come
About a man you met in Eccles who...

Swans

Not many see the white swans.
Vagrants at road-ends have
Or, waiting for shift-end,
Machine-minders staring
At dereliction through the blank panes.

Not many hear them. Soiled
Drunks have whom the cold wakes
Early lying curled;
Or, nearly sleeping, the innocent
Lovers. After birdsong

That is the kindest light.
Through silver grey, through rose
Across our malignant city
The heavy birds strain
In this season, about this hour

Little above roof-tops
Rapid, whistling, intent,
Steadily clouting the air.
Pity them should they flag
For where is there a meadow

Or any habitable water
And where, landing or falling,
When the day hardens and we
Come down the roads will they
Avoid our fatal notice?

Watching for Dolphins

In the summer months on every crossing to Piraeus
One noticed that certain passengers soon rose
From seats in the packed saloon and with serious
Looks and no acknowledgement of a common purpose
Passed forward through the small door into the bows
To watch for dolphins. One saw them lose

Every other wish. Even the lovers
Turned their desires on the sea, and a fat man
Hung with equipment to photograph the occasion
Stared like a saint, through sad bi-focals; others,
Hopeless themselves, looked to the children for they
Would see dolphins if anyone would. Day after day

Or on their last opportunity all gazed
Undecided whether a flat calm were favourable
Or a sea the sun and the wind between them raised
To a likeness of dolphins. Were gulls a sign, that fell
Screeching from the sky or over an unremarkable place
Sat in a silent school? Every face

After its character implored the sea.
All, unaccustomed, wanted epiphany,
Praying the sky would clang and the abused Aegean
Reverberate with cymbal, gong and drum.
We could not imagine more prayer, and had they then
On the waves, on the climax of our longing come

Smiling, snub-nosed, domed like satyrs, oh
We should have laughed and lifted the children up
Stranger to stranger, pointing how with a leap
They left their element, three or four times, centred
On grace, and heavily and warm re-entered,
Looping the keel. We should have felt them go

Further and further into the deep parts. But soon
We were among the great tankers, under their chains
In black water. We had not seen the dolphins
But woke, blinking. Eyes cast down
With no admission of disappointment the company
Dispersed and prepared to land in the city.

Islands

1. *Bracken*

There were sheep then, they pastured on the little islands,
We took them there by boat. But the grass has gone
And the fold my father's father built with his bare hands
Here at high water has also gone. One by one
All his fields have gone under the ferns again
And now it is hard for you to see how it was then.

Bitter, unharvested, deeper than children,
The ferns rise from high water over the wall.
The fields drown; the swinging gate is fallen
And ferns break round the posts that stand as tall
As men. But from the spring you climbed this way
After the spilling water-carts on a hot day.

You would not think we had any open ground,
But we did. We called it Plains. There was space
For all the island to be sitting round
Watching the tennis or the cricket. Our playing-place
Has gone the way of the fields and I shouldn't know
Where to look for the pitch and the court now.

Sunk flourishing in depths of bitter green
The little islands are lost to us already.
We watch from boats the rats going hungry between
Waste and waste. Remember for our sakes quickly
Where the sweet water places were and when
And by whom the fields were first rid of their bracken.

Sometimes in summer we made ourselves a bed
Under the ferns, where we should never be found,
And looked up through the lovely green at the sky and said
That we were at the bottom of the sea and drowned.
I believe sometimes we slept, but the afternoon
When we woke again was still no further gone.

We lie on the harbour wall and peering down
Where the wrack heaves and hideous claws feel
After food, we see the clouds that do not drown
In pathless water with all of our things lost but sail
Untouched through the coral and the salt flowers
Through the places of this island that once were ours.

2.

At blown cockcrow, hearing the driven sea,
You remember the rattling sash, starlight
Surviving faintly on the looking-glass
And the islands troubled with a ceaseless crying.

Scheria, kind to strangers, wept for her ship
Sunk by God unjustly; for the *Schiller's*
More than three hundred souls there were many in
Two continents weeping; and everywhere

For the sailors of our wars, numberless
Mothers' sons who have rolled in without faces.
Indifferent Hermes conducted them all.
The sea turns and its creatures hunger. Soon

Everything lies under the mercy of day.
The surface flickers with scared pilchards.
Light, above all the light. And the sea comes,
At sunny tide-flow the plucked, the smitten sea

Comes running. The wind then, high-ridden by
One nonchalant gull, batters the opening
Eyes of the sun with water. Far-reaching,
Iridescent, the white surf comes and comes.

Children are playing under a rainbow
On Pool Green; or behind Innisvouls,
Delighted in a rocking boat, they stand
Outstaring the ancient quizziness of seals.

3.

Our child when we came looking and calling after her
And had come through marram and sea-holly to the dunes' crest
When we stood crushing in our fingers plucked samphire
Looking still further and calling and saw her at last

She was remote and small on an almost island
And turned away, at tide-flow, but our fear was less
Of the sea already parting the cord of sand
Than that she was so small and averted from us.

We ran heavily, the white sand sank us in,
But through the neck of the place stole then like bird-stalkers
Over the flat wrack that popped and stank in the sun
Towards her kneeling before big granite chairs

Gently stroking for shells. When she turned and looked up
And showed us wordless in her palm the fissured cowrie
The spiralling white horn of wentletrap
And scallops smaller than her smallest nail then we

With our looks put upon her the fear of death
And the ownership of love. Between our tall shadows
She walked to the safe beach down the snake path
Already sunk over ankles in warm shallows.

Gratefully then the weed rose in the sunny water
And swirled as it liked and flowed and the bright shell
Hoards sparkled before the thrones without her
Who stood between us watching, waiting for tide-fall.

4. *The Drowned*

Flat calm. The ships have gone.
By moonlight and by daylight one by one
Into a different world the drowned men rise
But cannot claw the sleep out of their eyes.
None such can know the bigger light from the less
Nor taste even the salt. Their heaviness
By no means may be leavened. Now they live

As timbers do where shipworms thrive
Only in what they feed. Strange things engross
The little galleries of thought after the loss
Of breath. The white clouds pass, but still
The drowned increase upon the senses till
The moon delivers them. On islands then
Seeing the lovely daylight watchful men
Come down and haul these burdens from the waves
And slowly cart them home and dig them graves.

5.

The trees here, though the wind leave off, never unbend.
Likewise when he sat the stick retained
The shape of the sixty years he had limped and leaned.
He would haul from under the bed with the crook-end

His bundle of photographs and the soldier's pay-book,
The usual service medals and a card or two in silk.
The marriage bed was draped to the floor like a catafalque
And he hauled the War from under it. And when he spoke

Of the craters at Ypres he used the pool on Pool Green
As measure, and the island's entanglement of brambles when
He spoke of the wire. He rose, drinking gin,
Massive, straighter than his stick, and boys were shown

At the hoisting of his trouser up the sunless calf
A place that shrank like Lazarus from being raised,
A flesh the iron seemed only lately to have bruised.
And if one, being bidden and not in disbelief,

Put in the hand to prove him right who bet
That he was past hurt there – probing appalled
In that still weeping place the fingers rolled
Wondering between them an angle of iron grit.

For year by year his flesh, till he was dead,
Evicted its shrapnel, as the living ground
Puts out for the Parson or the Schoolmaster to find,
Scouring at leisure, another arrow head.

6. *Spring Tide*

The summer moon was terrible. It beamed
Like Christ on Lazarus. Nobody now,
In daylight, can distinguish what he dreamed
And what he saw, in night-clothes at the window.

It was like All Souls when everything lost
And the smothered dead struggle to rise. Around
Midnight the moon hauled hand over fist
And sheet by sheet the waters were unwound.

But nothing was recovered. Still the sand,
That we saw white and phosphorescent, levels
The slopes and pleasant laps of land
And stops the doorways and the fires and wells.

The curlews cried like springs starting to run.
Then sleep began to fill us and we felt
A weeping rise and flow. Now in the sun
The sea is brimful and our cheeks are wet and salt.

7.

Sheer nowhere: the land
Ends, the rocks pile dumbly where they fell,
And hold for any life nearer to ours than lichen
There is none; the useful
Wood of wrecks whitens beyond our reach.

Rain passes, rain on the sea, and sweetens
With all its copious fall
By not one measurable jot the expanse of salt.
Clinging to islands we
Camping with our dead around a sunken plain

Such as we are, late on,
Want above all things passage to one another,
Aid and the sharing of wells
And not to swell our bitterness beyond
The normal allocation of tears.

Journey

1.

Someone at least reading about beauty in a room
Above the city has turned from the lamp once having heard
Her step behind him on the creaking board and until
Morning then and until, close in the eaves, birds woke
He was allowed to lie on the narrow bed with her
Under the maps that papered the sloped ceiling
Embracing her freely and planning with her journeys.

2. *Locus Amoenus*

One read of the place where the covert mound rose
   Flanked by slopes, and clear water
Issued below for thirst and the excited mind
   And the senses equally were delighted.
One read of that pleasant place in the writers of pastoral
   And imagined its charms scattered over an earth
Less than so beautiful, and thinking never to come there
   Did: and found it surpassed their praises.

3. *Musée du Louvre*

These courtiers in a wood have come upon her
Rising before them moonlike in a clearing.
She strikes their eyes, their hands are all upraised
At the light she sheds upon them from her scallop.
Far inland henceforth, deep in the heart's covert,
Closing their eyes they will always hear the sea.

4. *Musée Rodin*

They saw the flgures of Fugitive Love and supposed them
   Wrought to the condition of subtility
By one another's hands: she streams away
   And the soul may be seen, playing upon her limbs.

The hotel bed was bordered with a mirror
    Where they reviewed those figures, curious
What novel disposition of themselves
    Would lend their evanescence form.

5. *Chartres and Avignon*

One could not look through it nor did the light
    From outside enter as light of day
But passed inward in the form of a persuasion
    That love hungers and will be filled by
No dexterity. That was the window of Mary,
    Of post coitum tristis. Waking
In Avignon he saw her beside him sleeping with
    The sheet thrown off, arms and throat
Already burned from travelling. The dirty pane
    Showed a blueness under which the town
With sprinkled gutters foretasted the dust
    And thin shade under walls at noon.

6. *Gothic or Classical*

Reading that in the depiction of the female body
North and south of the Alps there were two traditions
By stages night after night in disreputable hotels
North and south of the Alps he examined whether
She approached more nearly the Gothic or the Classical
Bearing in mind from Paris a certain Venus
As far as Florence where a lascivious Eve
Displayed her teeth-marks in the bitten apple.

7.

The mind then seems to become the burning point
    Of the other senses, when by day
Arches are seen and one's delight converges
    At their tips and down the aisles, and when
In darkness are corresponded all parts having stiffness
    Actual or potential, likewise
All declivities and entrances and more are devised
    And the mind then is the glass, burning.

Bluebells

But then her name, coming to her averted
And more than waist-deep in the ground's embrace,
How queer it sounded, like screaming swallows,
Like bats hurting her ears. Still, she turned

And lifted her face to the rim of beech-light
And the leaf-sieved sky. And again her name
Came down the slopes to her, tugging like grief
With little cries. So she was drawn. The blue ground

Let go of her in a white furrow and where
She had entered at the horseshoe's opening
Now she began in earnest her long haul
Against the streams, ascending slowly by

Degrees of blue under the cavernous light,
A floppy corpse of flowers on her left arm
With midnight hair, with blue dark thoughts, with white
Uprooted feet. Standing in the shallows,

Black to the waist, cradling the lolling doll,
She had no sight nor sound of her lost name.
Her bluebell lips, smiling at nobody,
Clouded the cold air with a breath of roots.

Autumn Lady's Tresses

In late summer the Lady's Tresses
Spiral to light leafless and stand
Almost as bare rods. But flowers
Proceed upwards by an unbraiding or as
When the wind frays
The scything edge of a wave. Thyrsus,
Snake of ivy. Flowers
Without energy of colour, at the least remove
From the stem's green. Torch-flower,
Faintlight, but prized by finders
As much as wentletraps
The white unicorn
The winding stairway shell.

Autumn Crocuses

The naked boys, entering the light,
Their root-whiteness suffuses upwards with a colour. Then,
So long as they hold the sun's eye,
Light through and through and barely tethered,
They stand hovering. They die
When they empty of sun, sleeves
Of their life lie on the soil crumpling.

Sunflowers

Stems wrist-thick,
A pulse of plant-blood;
Faces puffing like the four winds,
A hot light. Sunflowers in the days
When they wear the aureole of power,
The licks of flame,
They lap furiously at the sun
With rasping lion-tongue leaves. But they die
As big men do whose bodies the life finds heavy, they loll
And blacken like the crucified. At evening
You will hear them in the garden flapping their rags
Groaning to fall from the fences
Flat over the grass.

Tree in the Sun

This morning the tree shed
Leaves. There wasn't a breath of wind, not
A leaf stirred on the stem
But fell for an hour or more
After the frost last night the tree stood in the sun
And the leaves fell, there wasn't a moment
When any less than hundreds were falling and neither torn
From where they held nor in their fall
By the least wind deflected as when a day falls still
And the sky silently snows so they
Were shed but it was in the sun
They fell after what cold
In the body of the tree after the withdrawal of
The lifeblood to the heart no longer held
Themselves no longer adhering when the frost relaxed
The dead leaves fell for an hour or more.
Weakened by the sun after that night
The tree shed leaves.

Song of a Woman at the Year's Turning

My children were conceived in February.
I fall in love under the hesitant light
At the year's first singing. Snowfalls
Come like reprieve, like more and quieter sleep;
Lie everywhere in a kind prevention.

Snow on my hair. It must have seemed like grey,
Like ash for a moment. But come the shining sun
Winter collapses off the necks of daffodils;
The crocuses melt, they glow like spar. My hair
I feel jet-black and jewelled with water.

What will not open, what will not rise again
The year leaves for dead. Under that law
The helpless birds sing. What will not turn
And flow now singing will be hung
Like cadavers when the flood falls. I sing.

The purple crocuses open on an iron ground.
They have a frail centre. Birds whistle
Among their frozen dead. Trembling at heart
I shall be bold as purple, unbow like daffodils
And show my wintered face to the new sun.

Atlantis
(for Lotte and Hugh Shankland)

It dies hard, the notion of a just people;
   The wish that there should have been once mutual aid
Dies very hard. Through fire, through ghastly ash and any
   Smothering weight of water still we imagine
A life courteous and joyful; see them lightly clad
   Loving the sun, the vine and the grey olive.
Over the water, from trading, they come home winged
   With sails, their guide and harbinger the white dove.

I.

The sea suddenly stood up vertical, sky-high,
Bristling with the planks of their peaceful ships.
The earth roared like a bull. They said Poseidon,
Breaker of lintels, was shaking them. There was fire too
Glaring like a red eye. But the unkindest
Was of all the four elements the purest
And to breathing man his being: the air
Clagged and precipitated in cankers of pumice
And thereafter for weeks in a fine dust.
Wherever the living air was welcome now
Ash entered and the hearts of houses ceased;
Their eyes, hurt by blows, were quite extinguished;
Their mouths, agape, were stopped. Ash filled
And softly embedded household pots, shrouded
Frescoes of air-breathing dolphins. Who survived
When the sun had wept and blinked its eyesight clear
Lame in the lungs saw only dust
Lying now quiet as snow. One inch of such –
That is from nail-end to the knuckle of the thumb –
Will render infertile the fruitful, the man-nurturing earth
For perhaps ten years. To them now kneeling on rock
Who had salted no fields, burned no olive groves
And poisoned nobody's wells, there remained no rod
To sound the ells, the fathoms, the generations of ash.

II.

How deep below? None of the warring nations
Had length of chain to fathom at what depth
Atlantis lay. Nobody anchored there. But then –
In the days of death by impalement or the ganch
When Christian citizens of Candia ate
The besieging Turk – with a roar, witnesses say,
Like innumerable bulls, the sea, or the earth
Under the waters, rendered up to the surface
A new island, called nowadays *Kaimeni*,
The cinder. On Santorini the common people,
Scratching a living in the old ash and pumice,
Remembered Kalliste and watched and prayed. But a scholar,
A believer in Atlantis, when the steam had thinned
Pulled out alone in a small boat. How great
Must have been his disappointment if he thought
Some glimmer of Atlantis might be vouchsafed him
(Who had done no especial wrong in wicked times)
If he hoped for some however dim intimation
Of their lost lovingkindness and wisdom: he saw
Only black smoking slag and ash, and smelled
An intimation of Christian Hell. Also
The hot sea soon uncaulked his punt and rowing
Desperately heavily for home he sank
In depths well known to be unfathomable.

Chronicle

Scabby with salt the shipwreck wondering
Upon what shore, among what manner of savages
He was tossed up, found himself received
With a courtesy near to veneration. Lies
Were ready on his tongue but he found
His rescuers, his hosts, discreet or indifferent
And asking nothing. Only once he was bathed
And dressed in clothes held by for the occasion
There was a pause, a silence, and his fear returned
Imagining sacrifice. Solemnly, deferring,
They led him into the church. The congregation
Was the island's marriageable girls. He must choose,
They said, one for his bride. Any stranger
Showing himself indignant or lascivious
Heard behind him the whetting of knives. The wise man
Walked modestly two or three times
The length of the aisle and among the girls after
The heart's true inclination made his choice.
A priest of the church married them there and then.

Next morning early with a harder courtesy
He was fetched aboard a manned ship and so
Passed back into the sea-lanes. Some thus restored
Put off the escapade, some boasted and some
Wandered thereafter for the one bride. She
According to the custom of the island was courted by the best
And if she were seen to have taken the stranger's seed
Then by the very best, and married in her third month.

The second husbands shone like full moons
In reflected sun, their stepchildren
Were called 'the strangers' and enjoyed
Love and privileges above the rest. The boys
Grew proficient with boats, eyed the horizons
And one morning departed, courting shipwreck. The girls
Excited a restlessness but themselves
Waited, knowing they were most likely to be chosen
When out of the sea one morning a salt man crawled.

Sunium

Dawns may be rose and dove-grey
Evenings blue-black like Persephone
Lovely. But the culmination at noon
At sheer midsummer
That is incomparable.

Remember the bay, the water clear
As nectar in a calyx. There the sun
Brought our perception of carnal life
To the burning point.

Then the horizons had no attraction
There was no drowsiness, we watched
And bathed and sweetened the mouth with fruit.

Where promontories embrace an arena of sea
At noon the bivalve opened
The mollusc wings
The lips.

Lasithi

Lasithi: notable for windmills. Summits are
    The petals of Lasithi and their snow
Streams underground. Ten thousand mills, sailing like toys,
    Crank it to surface into troughs. At dawn
The families come down to a lake of mist. Women
    In black unmoor and swivel the bare crosses
To feel the wind. The rods blossom and in its throat
    A well reaches for water like a man
Strangling. It mounts like birdsong then – oh lovely work
    Of slowly scooping sails – it fills the reed,
The wells respire, the cisterns wait like mares and when
    In leaps, crashing like laughter, water comes,
A full wellbeing ascends and wets the walls and brims and
    Down the runnels like amusement overflows
Under the leaves, along the root-courses, and men
    Go about with hoes gently conducting it.

After the evaporation of the mist, under
   The sheer sun, under descending eagles,
Rimmed with snow, veined silvery with water and laced
   With childish flowers, the plateau works. The mills
Labour like lilies of the field, they toil and spin
   Like quivering cherry trees in one white orchard.

The Diktaean Cave

Children, attend. The myths are bloody. In this wet crack
For Mother Rhea, weary of fruitless birth, the Kouretes
Hid God the Usurper, little Zeus, from the cunning,
The child-swallowing Kronos – himself a son who for his mother,
Gaia, the Earth, weary of copulation, reaped from his father,
Vast Ouranos, the parts necessary with a jagged sickle.

The cry a hurt sky makes echoes for ever.
His fading semen splashed Heaven. Seaborn
Of the rosy froth where the unspeakable fell, our fierce
And gentle need grew. Blow out the candle. Darker
Than this and unimaginably deeper is Tartarus where grown
Zeus confined outwitted wily Kronos, having exhumed

Vigorous brothers and sisters from his guts. Zeus lived
The life of Riley then in the upper air, with clouts
Of thunder and strokes of the rod of lightning lording it;
And pressed divinity small into the bull, the swan, the eagle,
The golden dancing gnats, when tugged by Love, the immortal,
For one of the black earth's mortal sons and daughters.

A Relief of Pan

Standing behind you in the looking-glass
I saw my foolish admiration cross
Your own dispassionate appraisal of your dress.
I met your eyes, I saw you wished me gone,
I thought of that man by the Zappeion
Who likewise could not let you be in peace.

I had gone looking for a sanctuary of Pan
Along the dry Ilissos, you by the drinking-fountain
Sat eating cherries. I had gone
Looking unsuccessfully for a relief of Pan and he
Meanwhile, your gentleman of the Zappeion,
Was proffering you his member round an ilex tree.

Brother of mine, the Nymphs will not come down
To dead Ilissos, nor can you watch at home
A girl before her glass from nakedness become
Clothed like a stranger at the drinking-fountain
Nor watch her put off every ornament again
Saving a jewellery of cherries. I can,

I do. Yet I imagine being found
One day in shrubs below her window or by stairs
She might descend or shuffling after her in queues,
Eyes down, with cunning mirrors on my shoes.
I think it will amaze the officers
To learn what lady I have importuned.

Perdita

The brusqued sun returned, but milder, as
Through leaves over water, and silence too,
After the sprung lock, a clamour of birds
On the lake in the heart's forest settling.

Then nothing was between them but her bed
And that narrow. Come near to either bank
And staring neither saw when they began
At the throat the undressing very much of

The other's appearing nakedness since the eyes
Across the pause held them to their purpose
By force of looking face to face. Only
When she reached for the counterpane he saw

How bare her hand was and how thin her wrist
When she took off the covers and they stood
Shivering and unable to get breath
Beside a girl's sheets who with solemn dolls

Behind thin flowery curtains lessening
The strongest light had owned, until he backed
With pressing hands the blank door to, a room
As still as the heart pool of a forest.

Talitha Cumi

1.

Lazarus was heavy but she, little sister,
When he spoke to her softly in the common speech
She sat up beckoned by his little finger
Puzzled to be present at so important a *lever*.

They gave her milk to drink in her usual bowl.
Her lip took a white moustache. She made
Crumbs on the counterpane thoughtfully breaking bread.

2.

Sweet breath. She amused herself
Clouding her mother's mirror and with finger-tips
Then causing her re-appearance. Light
In a black grape held between finger and thumb
This pleased her too, and squinting at the sun
To discern its heart of darkness, and on her tongue sometimes
Curiously she felt for bitterness in honey.

3.

In dreams she was trailed again through the clear void
And caused the unborn to appear
Twinned with the dead. They seemed
A poppy-head bursting slowly or
The milky river of stars. They hung
Upon her when she returned
Like rime. She sat up thoughtfully
Against a hemisphere of Persephone blue
In which the comets and the little moons were vanishing.

4. *Glossolalia*

She sank or swam. Her father's pier of knowledge
Reached nowhere in that sea. He watched. She drowned
And surfaced, crying out and babbling in a language
High in rapid vowels, a tongue attuned

To pleading, like none he knew. The lamp held
Towards her eyes showed him himself unseen;
And pressing her cold hands he was only chilled
And could not wake her. She had lost her own

True intonation and having passed below
A surface spoke refracted. He feared that there
She had been loved at once and was missed now
And Death came pestering and questioning her,

A mistress of his tongue, and swore she lied
When she denied all knowledge of his seed.

5.

Within a month then came
Her first issue of blood. She feared
Another leaching of her strength but this
Was only the moon's small opportunity for life
Spent by her woman's body. Still
She lamented the going of her blood as though it were children.
Her heart was anxious like a linnet in a mine.

6.

O Kore with the little hurting breasts
Your elders' eyes are on you worse than mirrors.
Men waver in their looks when you put down
Your childhood one day like a doll and take
It up again the next with lavish love.
The women soon, too soon in their own lives,
All winter long lament Persephone,
Calling on God to send us a saviour,

A radiant child, they coax you out of the dark
Like pale narcissi. Returning girl
Our love of beauty and our fear of death
Oppress you worse than clouds. Look for a clearing
Ankle-deep in red anemones and pool
Your innocence with some ardent fumbling boy.

7. *Chanticleer*

The child's familiar whose stabbing beak
Tickled her palm for crumbs, the strutting lord
And master of a few hens in the little yard
Had never so woken her. The cock's head broke

Like bedlam through the tympanum of sleep,
Suffused, red-lappeted, with a wicked eye.
She saw him swell upon the eastern sky,
Showing the rose, the red and gold, and step

From the sea like God, crowing, splashing salt,
Turning the globe with claws. Her Chanticleer,
Her little favourite, she felt him sear
The dew away and savagely exult.

He had become a lord of thorns and a lord of spurs,
Of thorns flowering, of spurs raking his rivals
Until they streamed. There were no other pools
On the dry ground. The dew had gone and hers,

She thought, was the only charity left to the hard
Flamboyant earth and the brilliant salt sea.
Chanticleer stamped and rioted in the sun and she
Hid from him like the lidded well in the yard.

8.

Reluctant child. The family have gone
Calling for her to follow, climbing the fernhill.
Everyone has gone. But she still kneels
And strokes the shingle with her finger-tips for one
More augur, wentletrap or cowrie shell.

Mist. The familiar fernhill enters the sky.
The levels flood. The herd of tumuli,
The graveyard and the little islands
Lift from a drifting ground. The smothered sea
Creeps from oblivion in long winding bands.

Emerges. Breathes. All things become their ghosts.
The sun dissolves. But there are gaps of lightness against
A shoulder or between disappearing mounds
And dunes of the cliff-hill. Like a finger-post
High on the borders of daylight somebody stands

Singular on this island without trees
Calling a version of her name. But she is on hands and knees
Over a pool of shells and if she hears or sees
She pays him no attention. She may be sure
That more than once he will turn back for her.

The drowned are lowing in the fog. Come along,
She remembers them calling. She blinks the wet from her lashes
And sees a white sun shrinking and distending
And someone, stark as a post, more urgently beckoning.
Clutching her shells she begins the trudging paths.

Love of the Dark

We loved the rain, it bathed our minds to think of
The replenishing rain. On a morning then
The cloud had lifted and we saw the whiter
Splash of the stream at the cwm mouth and the wall

Through which the bracken trickled. Behind that dyke
Ownerless herds of fire cropped, unhousing
Little birds but leaving springs in hoofmarks and
On a craterous level above two valleys

The lake where once in a cotton grass summer
White gulls lifted quietly from the surface
And we undressed to bathe. I showed you afterwards
Blood on a stone, feathers and a bridge of bone.

Love of the dark, love of the falling silent
Of everything but the stream...We left the road
At nights, we trespassed over the properties
By the white clue of the climbing stream, by red

Lanterns of rowan. Above the stepping falls
Under the lintel of the lion-gate fold
And through a hogg-hole in the cyclopean wall
We entered our sleep like children. Hand in hand we

Ran some distance to the last skyline. The lake
Still lay in a sun- and moonlight at a time
Of the soft drifting of cotton grass or when
Ice clouded over our full crater of rain.

Moon

Under compulsion when the moon turned murderous
Coldly we walked out during the white hours
Who should have kept ourselves indoors for warmth
Asking of one another only mercy.

Sweetheart, I pleaded, under this hag moon
We must say nothing and look upon nothing.
Come in and sleep now or we shall convert
Our universe to ash and ice and stone.

Her hung and bitter face setting against me,
Look everywhere, she said, once and for all
And speak of everything and show me if you can
Some love still living under my truthful moon.

Turning to look I gave our fields to ash,
I creased the brows of hills with lines of stone,
I struck the wincing surface of our lake,
I wrinkled every stream. In silence then

Standing triumphant by the sobbing ice
I cupped my hands in trickling dust for her
Whom fever shook. Moon love, she said,
This being done how will you warm me now?

Red Figure Vase

Black where he is now who drew them, lightless
    My love, and where they are and all those
Like them, the youth and the girl, and where we
    Shall be, over the curve no sun,
No star ever rising. Black. See how they shine,
    Their fired bodies. Smiling she curves
Ascendant daylight over him to quench
    With her cone his standing torch. That done
Were they living they would sleep as we do
    Sightless, enfolded warm, on black.

FROM **MADDER**

(1987)

I mean the Dyer's Madder, *Rubia tinctorum*, that used to be cultivated extensively in Europe, especially in southern France, where it was called *garance*. The dye they got from it was a deep red, but the plant itself, a straggling, hairy and sharp-leaved plant, is dark green in colour. The flowers are small and yellow, the berries as they form pass from green through red to black, and when ripe they are juicy. The roots are the thing, that is where the redness is, in the thick, proliferating, energetic roots. Madder was planted in July and harvested in November of the following year. It was cleansed of its earth, then hung for months to dry; then ground to a serviceable powder in mills. This powder needed to be used within a year, before its virtue diminished.

Garance occurs as a measure of redness in troubadour poetry. 'His face went redder than madder,' they might say – for shame, perhaps, or love or anger. The powder was used against poisons and to heal a wound. And in 1737 an English surgeon by the name of Belcher fed madder to a pig and turned its skeleton red. He fed some to his chickens and turkeys too, and on the third day they were thoroughly red, in bone and tooth and claw. This Belcher fellow made me think of Orpheus.

Adam confesses an infidelity to Eve

I dreamed you were stolen from my left side
And woke hugging the pain. There in our room
Lit by the street lamp she appeared to me
Like something pulled from the earth. She is bulb-white;

Her shadowy place as black as wet moss
Or the widow spider. Believe me
She flattened my raised hands. She gripped
The cage of my heart between her knees,

Gluttonous for mandrake, and fed then,
Crammed her nether mouth, so rooting at
My evasive tongue I feared she would swallow it.
Curtained together under her hair

Only when she rose from drinking
And rolled and bucked as though I were reined
Did I see her face, like a slant moon,
Her eyes smudged and cavernous, her mouth bruised.

She cried like a seal. When she bowed down
Her brow on mine as savages pray
Enshrining my head between her forearms
Then, I confess, feeling her cold tears

I lapped them from her cheeks and let her rest.
My seed ran out of her, cold. On the street
Hissing with rain the lamps were extinguished.
You, when I woke, lay hooped on my left arm.

Orpheus

Styx is only a stone's throw from here,
From anywhere, but listen: here
You can catch Eurydice's scream
And count how long before she hits

That water. Afterwards
He mooched through such a landscape:
The sun was low in the wrong hemisphere
And hurt his eyes, the birds

Were plump and garish and their chorus,
Mornings, a lascivious rattle;
His familiar trees – the willow,
The poplar – were all yellow

But as blanched as what he had seen of the damned
Were the unfamiliar. Through a willow fringe
He watched the people who looked accustomed
Taking their walks and seemed

To himself only as she had seen him last:
A silhouette. Dearest
I think it was such a flight of poplars
He entered finally and turned

At the dazzled end, calico-thin,
And saw his red griefs coming for him. Listen:
The whisper of Styx, her scream
On which his slung head, singing softly, homes.

Siesta

On edge again, over nothing
Near to tears, when the curtain rattles
And only the warm wind enters
And not the scent of rain, he sees

Garance (it is the name of a flower)
Leaving the water as he approaches
And putting on her clothes.
She ages rapidly around the eyes.

Any more songs, he cries, any more stories,
Any more entering as sisters arm in arm
And leading me to believe you in the shuttered room
Barefoot on the marble

And you can look for me in spots of blood
Across the ponds of cotton grass.

Yseut

The white company of the lepers
Whom we pitied a little and left food for
Whose myxy eyes skenned down the misery slit
At our virgins receiving the Saviour

They have a new white queen
And we go out less, nobody picnics, theirs
Are all the pastorals of this season.
What have we done, what have we let happen?

The King's glee was shortlived.
When the gate banged and he heard their jubilation
He turned the colour of the underside of fungus
He was of a weeping texture, feverous.

One of us shot into the pack today
When they were feasting with their blunt hands
At the cressy well. Now their bells
And clappers are louder and we are nervy.

The King stands looking at the lonely post.
He wants her back again in the opened cloak
Of faggots: to see her soul like a water-baby
Scat heavenwards through the smoke.

He will put a bounty on his Queen
And send us hunting the scuttling herds.
He sweats at the thought that she will give birth.
Her progeny, his doing, will people the earth.

Ignis

This land was crazy with the loves of Christ:
Straight running of the lame, a dance,
The multitude picnicking.

Ones he unfastened the mouths of
And got their tongues going
They ran about charged with the word 'ignis',

They babbled to right and left of an interdiction,
Their mouths overflowed
With tongues, with lucifers, and ones

He took out the darkness under the lids from
And told them not to tell
They saw the light of the eyes into everything.

He said to follow his trespasses
And convert the charnel lands
Where our brothers and sisters still go cutting themselves.

Martyr

This man, if we can call him that, this foetus,
This white larva, he was there at the Dry Tree
As a merry child, a pig-minder, when Christ,
So we believe, (the dates do tally) did that
Trick with spittle and two dead eyes and the sight
Or was it the ensuing loud hallelujah
Or being spotted in the stinking mayweed
Tugging away at himself no doubt among
Our burned-out necklaces and the handy stones
And Jesus telling him to cross his heart and
Hope to die if he told a soul about it
(Everyone did) and him telling his mam? It
Blew the wits of that doughty little witness
Of many occurrences on that bloody spot.
His mam never saw the stars of his eyes again.
She watched him curl and eavesdropped on his nightmares.
She even petitioned the travelling Master
To please come and wipe her little man's vision
Clean of the miracle. We reckon in his fist
(Observe how over the years he has eaten at it)
We'll find the crooked sixpence Jesus flicked him
When our blind brother saw the heavenly blue.

Oh, Jemima...

I was there, I was the man in black in case
His ticker burst, but I watched Jemima
Whom they were yelling at to look and the sweet thing
In boots sucked on her barley sugar and throughout
The uproar of the ducks and when our man was in
Rotavating the water with his white arms
And his legs were fighting one another she
Only did as she was bid and looked and of course
Never screamed nor covered her eyes nor wet herself.

She saw him crawl up the bank with muddy eyes
And weed on his tonsure and his busy-bee stripes
At half-mast, Flo handing him his glasses
And a cup of tea and Arthur a handkerchief and me
Going in with my little silver ponce to sound him out.

And I was there coming down from Ethel's bed
And the same little nod our Jemima gave
When they wrapped Uncle away I saw her give
That morning over her bowl when Flo's card came
Saying that Jim, the learner, the brave tryer,
Was took on the West Coast doing his few strokes
Up the Acheron, against its tide, into its freezing mouth.

Don't jump off the roof, Dad...

I see the amplified mouths of my little ones
And dear old Betty beseeching me with a trowel.
I am the breadwinner, they want me down of course.
I expect they have telephoned the fire brigade.

They have misinterpreted my whizzing arms:
I am not losing my balance nor fighting wasps
Nor waving hello nor signalling for help.
These are my props and I am revving up.

From here I have pity on the whole estate.
The homegoing lollipop lady regards me with amazement.
I shall be on the news. Lovely Mrs Pemberton
Will clutch Mr Pemberton and cry: It's him!

Ladies, I am not bandy, it is the footing I must keep.
My run-up along the ridge-tiles will be inelegant.
But after lift-off, breasting the balmy wind
And when I bear westwards and have the wind in my tail

Then what a shot I shall make, going for the big sun,
Over the flowering cherries and the weeping willows,
Beating along Acacia Avenue with a purpose
Towards the park and the ornamental lake.

The Meeting of God and Michael Finnegan in South Park

Sunday, early; foul with dreams
Entering the empty park between two bent railings
I found his crutches towards the bottom of the hill
Lying on the long undulations of grass
Like spars of wreck. So, I thought,
Michael has met God as he always said he would.

He will have dropped from them last night
Having swung this far out of the soiled city.
Here is his jagged bottle. This morning then,
Waking with scabby lips, he saw God walking in the park,
Dewy-grey, delighted by blackbirds and songthrushes
And the scent of the mown grass. Look, God said

To Michael Finnegan, how beautiful the city is,
The white spires, delicate as a moonshell,
Reaching from sleep into the soft blue daylight.
And see the well-spaced leafing trees: that copse
Through which is passing even now a frisson of joy,
That single poplar in a brave plume – and there

A damp place which is a beginning stream
To water the pale city. Begin again, said God,
Leave your crutches lying and no excuses. Don't,
For example, be telling me you must wait for the keeper
To let you out. My fence is vandalised
Where you came in and above, higher,

Passing that single and admonishing poplar,
That convocation of oaks, that company
Of beeches downed like youths in Homer,
Leaving behind and further and further below you
The city sparkling like a hoard of shells
You will find a gap I made for the convenience of the children.

So Michael Finnegan spewed up some green bile
And wiped his lips and saw blood on the back of his hand
And found his feet and climbed the long slope unaided
And far below him in the moonlike city
From towers, faintly, fell the notes
Of an hour that was still unearthly.

Don Giovanni: Six Sonnets

1. *Act 2 Scene 18*

When he had gone, burning in hell fire,
And the valet in black had drawn the cloth and they
Had sung the restoration of order in a choir
In separate silences they turned loosely away:
Facing a nunnery, marriage to a fool, marriage
To a woman in love and service more tedious.
He was their sun, his fist had held them, each
Released now travelled down a different radius.

Turning on a widening wheel, come spring
After a winter they will rake his fires to life
Under the heart's ash and his singing will begin again
Coursing through them like sap. Thirsting then, burning,
Servant, nun, husband, unloving wife
Will scan the linen for his last wine's stain.

2. *'How can men want wearisomely to philander?'*
LEPORELLO TO DONN' ELVIRA

Burgos is full of women and Burgos is only one
Of the cities of Spain full of women and Spain
Etc. They are a drop in the ocean
The thousand and three. And it's all labour in vain.
He's ladling at women with a sieve
And like the proverbial good shepherd he'll leave
The one to chase the missing ninety-nine
Up hill down dale in the wind and the rain
And lose the one. Lady, he never lets up.
The poor man hasn't had a holiday in years.
He sees himself as one of life's almoners
And bringers of sunshine, handing his loving cup
To rich and poor, fair and ugly, and the shriven
Kneeling with sinners for his French stick of heaven.

3. *Zerlina*

Waking this morning I was someone else:
A wife who knows she has conceived, but the shock
I felt under my heart was remembering how he struck
The strings with the backs of his fingers and my new pulse
Was the starting again of his singing in my veins
Sotto voce. I have gone about the house
And to and fro in the garden hearing his damned voice
All day under my clothes carrying his tunes.

He swung my soul, he showed me how they move
In very presence, those whom an innocent love
Flings to the dance. And I believed his tongue,
I swallowed him, we married there and then.
I am his lawful widow big with song.
I have danced all day, believing him again.

4. *Zerlina*

He had a house, if I would follow him in
He promised we should debate the old question
How many angels might dance on the head of a pin
He guessed in my case more than a million.
There was music for what we felt, he said,
But as yet no dance. I was to imagine
Things overlapping, things deeply interlaid,
Crown-knots of fire. His hand on mine,
Our fingers so interslotted that we could not tell
Left from right, his from mine. I was to dwell
As dance on the interleafing of warm waves
Over a sand bar, their passing through themselves,
Their continuing rippling on the tide that weaves
A depth of them in which the island dissolves.

5. *Leporello*

Forked in her moorish arches, standing sentry,
I watched the summer heavens teeming down;
I dozed under her generous balcony,
Dopey with orange blossom and moonshine,
Hearing their silly laughter above my head,
His rapier clattering to the marble floor,
Rustle and sigh of things of hers discarded,
A rose thrown over into my lamplight square.
When he came down I kissed his ungloved hands
And we escaped then through the skirting gardens.
Once, in the wolf's clothing, using his voice,
I drew his starved wife down. Inhaled the perfume
Of an amorous woman, saw the abandoned face
That hurt my eyes even through my borrowed plume.

6. *Donn' Elvira*

I see my face in the black window glass;
I touch my throat, feeling for Christ's chain;
I think of charitable casual women
Who at the throat begin to undo their dress.

Christ knows my visions and may forgive me them.
They are of women and my spouse in Hell.
They stand among their fallen clothes and smile
And show him their white places without shame.

I should have smiled, I should have had their ease.
My love was like the terror of the lamb
Under his knife. Don Juan never saw
Amusement at his passion in my eyes.
I am the widow of a man at whom
I never smiled as though I were his whore.

Confessional

Where, in a French church, stuck through
And dreaming of haymaking in Liebenau,
Should he go to die? Not in the lee of the altar
Nor spreadeagled under the tower.
He hid in the confessional and died seated
Leaning forward as though to the priest's ear.

Americans were brought in dead
And laid down the hollow nave to the altar steps
And from north to south on the transept
And peasants with faces like the Conqueror's
Embarking in their church windows made
A white cross over them with armfuls of June flowers.

The dead man from Liebenau sat still
Behind the curtain in the confessional
Pressing his open mouth to the grille.

Thoughts of the Commandant of the Fortress of St Vaast-la-Hougue

My boy keeps up appearances.
He props the dead soldiers in their embrasures
And fires their muskets from time to time.

By candle light in the nucleus
With a bitten finger I patrol our miles of walls
Hearing at every turn the claws of a grapnel
Or the moat bleeding away through a wound.

And what is worse: low tide when we
Padlock our throat and cordon the slit with salt
And the birds stalk over the foetid mud
Bayoneting the overturned soft crustaceans?

Or full: when we are brimming with fear
That our besiegers thus will fall quietly upon us
With the soft wings and the demon faces of moths?

They have surrendered oceans of freedom to beat these walls.
How furious will be their disappointment
After the falling silent of my ragged bird-scarer.

Pillbox

Dome of the sun. So we shall burn
Immured in a head, peering through hyphens.
Though we are prickly with angles of vision
An intelligence may calculate our blindspots
A hand rise out of the earth
To post us flames. Somebody squats
On the skull with a trepan
Where our flailing glances cannot dislodge him.
The surf is placid at nights
And soothing the scent of camomile.
We have nailed this coast. Buried to the eyeballs
We shall burn like lampions.
The quenching Atlantic will back away from us.

Nestor encourages the troops
(after Iliad *ii. 336ff.)*

My dears, you sound like little boys
Still pimply before they redden out
With bloodlust. Who promised then? Did not
We all with drink and a handshake
Cross our hearts and hope to die
For Agamemnon? Yapping, though we yap
Till kingdom come, will get us nowhere. Sir,

Lead them cheerfully back on to
The killing-ground and let
The one or two malingerers, the schemers
For early home-time, the impiously
Unwaiting to hear God's final word, let them
Drop dead. I personally
Believe we were given the nod and the wink
That day by Zeus. It lightened, did it not,
Righthandedly when we were boarding
Our snouted ships for Troy. Well then
For Helen's misdemeanours and your wasted years
Anticipate a just desert
Of married Trojan cunt. When we are in
And the pretty fires are burning and only toddlers
And snivelling old men encumber your knees
Remember then you thought of going home. However
If luxury to come (shitting on silks)
Will not embolden you try running and we,
Your lords, will stick you to the ships.

Garden with red-hot pokers and agapanthus

The link flowers that stood in a loose sheaf
Cock-red and yellow-wattled
A clear honey dabbling their waxy spikes

When you pushed open the gate in the garden wall
They dubbed your bare shoulder
When you went down the granite steps

Pushing open the gate that was always half-open
You agitated the flames and the embers
When you went down into the cool agapanthus.

The green iron gate was always half-open,
There were steps down. The agapanthus
Is shock-headed and slim. Love, through a caul,

Through slung cells dotted with life,
Through sunrises and rose
Windows of webs I watched for you climbing

Out of the place of quenched fires
Dew on your hair, your flinching shoulders
Touched with yellow pollen.

'Looking for nothing'

Looking for nothing but a place in the sun
We found the cricket-pitch that nobody
Finds by looking: an outfield head-high,
A plateau of curious topiary
And twenty-two paces of asphalt battened on
By gorse like sea-slugs. Over the boundary

The wind streamed downhill in a bright sunlight
Through choppy bracken with a watery din
And entered the sea. Wading in
We found the drinking trough of lichened concrete
Still holding water that had fallen sweet
Nowhere arable, nowhere beasts might feed.

We lay in the sun's cupped hands
By the undrunk water mouth on mouth
Below the cricketers' flat earth, beyond
Their lost sixes. We opened
Rapidly from diminutive springs, like breath
Surfacing butterflies wafted down the wind.

Sunset Shells

Sunset shells, of which there were millions
Banked at our bare feet, like a flint scraper
They fit exactly into an idle
Skimming grip between finger and thumb.

That day whilst the sun blew and the long-
Sleeved tide harped louder over the sandbar
Until the island was awash for the last
Half hour we were launching sunset shells.

Oh, we threw thousands, they saucered up and
Cut from under by the sunny wind
Each at its curve's high-point paused spinning
And was returned overhead into

The sea's incoming arms with a sound
Like kissing and floated briefly, we had
Behind us a flotilla of little
Sinking coracles and in the sky

Always any number climbing to
Their points of stall and boomeranging down
The windslopes. The sun laughed and the tide
Like clapping drew the last white curtains.

Oranges

I.

Mother has linen from the *Minnehaha*,
I bought the ship's bell for half a sovereign
From Stanley, our dumb man.
Everyone has something, a chair, a bit of brass

And nobody wakes hearing a wind blow
Who does not hope there'll be things come in
Worth having, but today
Was a quiet morning after a quiet night.

II.

The bay was coloured in
With bobbing oranges. What silence
Till we pitched into it
Knee-deep the women holding out their skirts

And the men thrashing in boats
We made an easy killing
We took off multitudes
And mounded them in the cold sun.

When Matty halved one with his jack-knife
It was good right through, as red
As garnet, he gave the halves
His girls who sucked them out.

III.

The beams we owe the sea
Are restless tonight but every home
Is lit with oranges. They were close,
She says, or else the salt

Had eaten them. Whose popping eyes,
I wonder, saw them leave
Roaring like meteors
When the ship in a quiet night

Bled them and they climbed
Faster than rats in furious shining shoals
In firm bubbles and what
Will tumble in our broken bay tomorrow?

Sols

(for Alice Thomas, in memory of her son,
my cousin, who died in 1943, aged three weeks)

1.

Planting is hard, so much stooping uphill,
But leisurely and we can lob
Some conversation over the high hedges,
Share forenoon in a strip of shade.

Picking is desperate though, the wind
Reaches in like a bear fishing.
We get them out earlier and earlier
Hurrying under frightful red skies.

The market demands it, however green
They are and tighter than shut beaks.
Packing them is a stiff business,
So many rods, box after box. Some die,

That's certain, die at sea, and what
Could we deal worse into the roofed homes
There to be broached behind drawn curtains
Than a Christmas box of sols

With wrinkled eyes that no one's hands
Taking them up or water will freshen?
The house had already imagined
The scent of gratefulness in every room

Which is the breathing again of sols
When a woman lifts them like a love child
Out of the ark that crossed the wolfish sea
From the world's end at the time of miracles.

2.

The harvests were golden once and every room
Of that formal maze had a fire of flowers
Whatever the weather constantly fuelled
With cradled armfuls. The little paths

Going through our roofless windy city
Like cracks in brickwork by two or three steps
At slits in the tall euonymus
Trickled with gold. The trundling carts

Climbed to the packing-house, the long shed,
Like royal hearses. From a broken rim
The harboured steamer received into her hold
The burden of busy gigs and launches.

3.

They worked all the hours God gave
They could never pick fast enough
The fingers of the women were raw with tying
They were minting gold
Hand over fist, the currency of grief,
And bloating the steamer with condolences.

4.

Christmas, and not a candle showing;
The steamer kept coming, the markets of London
Were lit with flowers, by grief's
Osmosis they were drawn

Through every capillary:
Down highways in a slow march
Sinuously through lanes and cricked
At stepping angles through the slums.

5.

Put off alone in a white ark
He scents the room like bread
Fresh on a board, like sols
In sparkling vases. But silence is natural
To the breathing of bread and sols and nobody
Pushing open the door ajar
On darkness would listen thus and crane
And tiptoe in and lean with an ear downwards
To be certain they still lived.

6. *Strafe*

Curiosity, since by daylight
He could never revisit the unroofed slums
To peer inside or glance at a slice of living-room –
Its tatters of floral wallpaper and dog's

Hind-leg of a flue – he never saw
In a winter daylight the exact layout
Of our cemetery fixed among the lines
Of railway, box-like factories and canal,

Never swooped low in the sparkling frostlight
To observe the neat little casts of the newest graves
And their cut flowers and perhaps a cortège
Pushing, as though congealing, through a back street.

So curiosity brought him low over the bulbfields,
Gentle township of evergreen walls,
Corrals of sunshine open to the sky
Whose goods nothing worse than a south-easter swipes.

And there were little people busy at the source of flowers
Who ran at his roar, dropping their burdens,
And hid where we look for shade.
He came in low, he saw their white faces.

7.

Since it is sleep that makes possible
The coming of the sackman, cherry-red,
Who can pass through soot with his white beard immaculate,
Sleep and the darkness, a black heaven,

A sheeted firmament, darkness in the attic,
Darkness in all the sleeping rooms,
The children are desperate to sleep and clench their eyes
Fearful they keep the red man listening at the door

Unable to enter, fearful he will turn on his heel
And shoulder the sack, but worse, almost,
Should he mistakenly believe their breathing
And enter the knowing darkness with effulgent whiskers.

8.

Concave over the magic box
My father holds his breath and a small soul
Has appeared in the Brownie eye. Then light
Admitted is severed with a click.

Soon I am entered in the quilted album
On the first black page. All babies look alike
But here is my name in small white capitals.
Ergo sum! My resting place

Is the Morrison built not to give
At the knees or cave in under
A rubbled house. It easily took
Your leaden grief in a box till he

Was sided away to a third-class plot
In the big necropolis
In perpetuity. Lid the cradle
And that is how it looked, with flowers,

In a blacked-out house when he had flitted through
The lit rooms, your cock sparrow.
But you had pictured him for ever.
As we go forward now

Print after print and you are saying what
He would have been, I blur with light
Like streetlamps when our eyes are wet
As if his ghost got in.

9.

Had he come down from the dark
Even three or four of the fifteen stairs
He could have looked into the living-room
And seen the fire and the lord of the fire:

Father in a long dressing-gown,
A shield on his arm, the black blower;
A sword in his hand, the silver poker;
Ushering the flames up. When Father kneeled

And tinkered with the damper
The flames became a quiet curtain
This side of which there was a smell of hot soot
And a trail of Woolworth's glitter.

Hugging the cornucopia,
The lumpy stocking from the bed-end,
Had he come in the table was laid for him
Its leaves extended as though for company.

Crusaders in a fort; a farm:
The lovable animals, the health of the green fields;
Houses, a lighted church, the whole world
Looped by a tremendous locomotive.

[St Martin's, Isles of Scilly / Salford 5]

Cold Night

We saw the pent fish redden the ice
In a Grecian park where the Cnidian
And Pan accustomed to nightingales
Stayed out all night with the owls.

The trees are brittle, the streams wrung dry;
The ice yelps at the least thing
Like a railway line; along
The scoured road there are drifts in a drove.

Drifts: they are water thrown
Under the undulating air, they are
The manifest line breath took
When the clouding water set. And we

Where are we? Listening to the owls
Or the ice or the rim of the moon:
Something that cries with little cries
Under the lake moon, under the ice

Where the drifts move in their shapes
Like seals or whales and sound
For one another down the bloodstreams
With a strange phoning, like owls.

'As though on a mountain'

As though on a mountain, on the sunny side,
The view over seven counties suddenly palled
And the stream we had bathed in, our loveliest,
We fell to damming so that not the least
Of relief could leak through, no not a mouthful;

As though downstream somewhere, still naked,
We seated ourselves on the two facing rocks
And made some conversation until the air tasted,
The shallows got tepid and our mouths dried up
And we listened to the waters piling behind our backs;

As though we joined hands then, still bleeding from the labour;
As though the waters broke; as though together
With rubble and furious fish and trees the chute
Of waters shovelled us off the mountain
Eating each other's heart in the mouth out.

To be honest, I'm losing my nerve. One day
We'll finish in town like that, on show,
A phenomenon come out of the sky, beastly,
My beautiful, ingrown, rooted through.

At Dinas

The sea runs, the long-haired breakers
Come on and on with a constant thunder;
They wear the pelts and manes of animals,
They show their throats.

At the sea's edge you look run to death,
You turn your face towards us shining with tears,
You seem to hang from your surrendering wrists;
But the sea lifts

As though you raised it. For if grief tears
The head back so will happiness, the throat
Intones and maybe your mouth's drowned
O is singing.

We three look monstrous, our heads so close
The blood beats through and across our open mouths
The wind howling. But thus we accompany you
With drum and flute.

Local Story

I.

When a tree falls
The rooty place
Is beloved of children.
We opened loaves
And fruit for one another;
At the tap-root
Drank a white drink.
All we asked was to flower
In one another's features
And be apportioned
Fairly below.

II.

To the black cwm
Through the sunny forest
By way of the stream.
Though I often turned
You continued following
Bare to the waist
You three were following.

A grey snow
Hurts in the cracks of the face
Long beyond spring;
Scree, wreckage,
A circling echo.
Where have I led you
Shivering?

III.

Reading the excreta
Of crows and foxes
We fell on whortleberries.
We had inky fingers
And the mouths of the drowned.

On a high headland
In a form of heather
We entertained the lord of the place
Old Proteus
With our curious love-knots.

The light changed
The hill stood up and brushed our picnic off.
God watched us out of sight with other clouds.
We were never hived
We were less than crumbs of pollen.

IV.

We lit a last fire with our swag of seed.
Under the coals
Among the kindling of splintered driftwood
It sang and cried.
We swallowed souls of firelight in our wine.

Mynydd Mawr

All night sopping up rain
At daybreak the wells of the hill opened
The animal in my crystal valley
Doled itself downstream more rapidly.

Everything flows, it must, the skull
That lodges in the stream exults
At the eyes and at the widened mouth. On Mynydd Mawr
A high wind bearing the law upon me

I let this house go, turning it
Into the rivers from the rainbow's end
Let go our beds and fires
The bowl of berries and the driftwood in arms

The holly, the harebells and the only rowan
And the long icicles brought home
I dealt them down the wind
I conjured everything out of me

Owls and curlews and a peck of jackdaws
And the tunes of dreams. Turning then
There was a steady scintillation
The wet was shining off every surface stone

As I came into the quick of the rainbow
Into the roar with widening eyes
And over my thin skin Mynydd Mawr
Flowed out of the sky, cold silver.

Swimmer
(in memoriam Frances Horovitz, 1938-83)

In summer the fires come and feed here
Like starlings. If the earth knew
She would feel a shiver of memory.
Ash on that crumpled ground.

The lake in a luminous silence, sunlight
Shed generally through the air,
A light of dreams; no lapping, shingle and
Water in a still seam.

Swimmer, the hills say, having come through ash
And snagging stumps and now
Idling on a warm surface to the midpoint
Naked, alone, try standing,

Swimmer, the sky says, tread water and feel
How thin the warmth is, thinner
Than the earth's burned hide, as thin as the Holocene
On Time's shaft and below

What a pull of cold, what colder than stone depths
Your feet are rooting in
And the cold rising as though cold were the sap
And blood of a new flower:

Death. Try calling a name, swimmer at the hub
Of a lake in a wheel
Of hills, your voice will flutter on the black slopes.
Kick, then, enjoy the surface.

Butterfly

A year and a day. Then too
There were daddy-long-legs wrecked on the flagstones
And ladybirds heading nowhere.

He offered me something in his closed hands
So suddenly my breath came with a scream.
He said was I frightened even of butterfly kisses?
Did I think he would feed me a spider?

He looked bound at the wrists
Until the flower of his hands opened
And he showed her spread and gave her up to the sky
With whole days still to live.

Fly away home: the poor shell creatures cannot
Nor can the crippled dancers lift
Off these immense piazzas.

'Then comes this fool'

Then comes this fool, muttering about freedom
And stands watching my hands and makes me nervous
And says there's a better game he knows with hands
And undoes everything, and what *he* does

Looks complicated, like a cat's-cradle,
And frail as a web and more and more like a rainbow
When he makes that wicked sign with his thumbs and fingers
And purses his lips and softly begins to blow.

And I'll set sail, he says, there's a nice breeze,
I'll probably be in paradise by tea-time.
I ask what the life expectancy of bubbles is.
They go far, he says. He says in the first dream

When I had hidden he was only passing
And kissed my whitened knuckles on the window bars.
I wonder how I undo what it was he did.
He will push off soon, muttering about the stars.

Mistress

Women whose hands know the feel of a baby's head
Push them confidently in among the melons
And their strong brown thumbs side by side,
Beautifully cuticled, feel for give on the crown.

That summer of the hot winds and the fires
The melons were sold split. He held me one
Before we had paid for it, before all the people,
To smell the inside of at its small
Opening fleur-de-lys and we went down
In a river of laughter between the banked stalls
Among all the people swinging our fruit in a net.

He made the cuts but I opened it
And for a moment my hands were a bowl of flames.
I served him cradles and the moons of nursery rhymes
And a family of rocking boats. We ate
And our mouths ran over with luscious smiles.

Then he closed my hands into a fist and held them shut.

'Wet lilac, drifts of hail'

Wet lilac, drifts of hail; everything shines
After the white rain, the gutters stream with seed;
Glistening in a fierce sun the road pitches
Downhill into an entrance of chestnut trees.

Tonight shall we cross the same meadow
And steal in the long gardens? I wore
Blossom in my hair, I wore a white dress,
I gave him my shoes to carry and ran away barefoot.

In love's month, after the first winter,
Apple trees revive in the memory of the dead
And they remember pink and white apple blossom
Flung down on the grass like a girl's clothes.

After a year the entrance is lit again
With high candles and the dead wait in the dark
For somebody coming, their flowers of hope
Plucking to nothing in fretting fingers.

My empty-handed love, someone will come
Soon bringing me armfuls of stolen lilac,
Sparkles of rain in his hair, and the black earth
Tonight when I run barefoot will quake with sobs.

Poplar

He slept at once as though
Escaping, he slid from my mouth
With a smile of thankfulness
And at the temple then his blood
Quietened upon my heartbeat, as though
The sea had pitched him far enough
And now withdrew, but I
Came to and heard
What I thought was a river
Passing overhead through our crown
Of leaves, I seemed
To be lying in a downpour, one
That drenched and blessed
My sleepy sub-self, the ground
Of me, and I wondered at
His fear of sadness
And of new desire like that
For snowy mountains rising again
Always too far distant,
I could conceive of none –
No thirst, no sadness, no distance –
My downpour could not answer.

Apples
(for my father-in-law on his eightieth birthday)

The daughter has a taste for sharp apples
And lolls in a fork, munching; little brother,
Blonder than corn, can dangle one-handed
Far out. Elsewhere, so I believe,

These things are forbidden, there is a scarecrow
And it is not you who strolls by
To see what the children are up to
But old Mr McGregor or God the Father.

112

On the lawn all you are judging
Is the likely parabola of apples when the tree
With a shout next fires one off;
You resemble a Green Man

Fielding eagerly at silly-point,
Your nettle-proof hands seem to be praying
Apples will fall. Those we miss
Bruise with a white spittle

And some my ring nicks, we lay them down
For immediate pies. In the apple light
Among the globes and leaves
The lucky children have ascended again

To the era of pure monkey tricks
Where lichen roughened us
And we were barked and greened. Our little Lob
Has stuffed his tee shirt full

So that I wonder, and perhaps you do too,
Who are four yards and forty years away,
Whether apples in a shirt
Have the feel girls have. Catching apples

And once my daughter's core
All afternoon I have been praising Eve,
The starred girl, the apple-halver,
Who has redeemed us from Mary-without-spot.

Pictures

Whether to take down the Kissing Swallows
And the Modigliani nude
And blu-tack something else there: a child,
Say, on fire and running towards us

Down a long road; or this little dot
Who bellywise looks almost bigger
Than her mother was; or any
One of those solemn witnesses we stand

In our photographs of a new mass grave
Like gentlemen in an old print
Modestly indicating by their smallness
Something phenomenal. The children

In this photograph from El Salvador
Are that international pair, a boy
And a little girl on a roadsign
Running, and below them, his head

In the gutter and his black blood
Being lapped by a row of dogs, on a road
Empty but for the photographer
A man has fallen among worse than thieves.

Amber Seahorse
(for Mary-Ann)

Europe is ripped through, my darling,
The resinous trees have little spastic arms,
The golden routes are leaden and the lap
He came from can't imbibe much more. I read

That the hippocamp is a sovereigne remedie
Against the byting of a madde dogge. Hold on
To him, it may soon come to that as
Every day they open up more badlands,

Burnish him, love, for some fluorescence
A while longer and note his canny eye,
His long shrewd nose and the springy tail
He rode the flood out on.

Traveller, bright thinker,
Remember the wreckage of the woman of Sindhos
Lying under glass like Snow White
And the finds where they were found:

Amber where the throat was, given her,
I think, and worn for love; a bowl
Lying in her vanished lap, her dusty
Hands had grasped it, proffering.

Eldon Hole

They fastened a poor man here on a rope's end
And through the turbulence of the jackdaws let him down
To where everything lost collects, all the earth's cold,
And the crying of fallen things goes round and round
And where, if anywhere, the worm is coiled.

When he had filled with cold they hauled him up.
The horrors were swarming in his beard and hair.
His teeth had broken chattering and could not stop
Mincing his tongue. He lay in the rope and stared,
Stared at the sky and feared he would live for ever.

Like one of those dreadful fish that are all head
They saw him at his little window beaming out
Bald and whiskerless and squiddy-eyed
He hung in the branches of their nightmares like a swede.
They listened at his door for in his throat

Poor Isaac when the wounds in his mouth had healed
Talked to himself deep down. It was a sound
Like the never-ending yelps of a small stone
Falling to where the worm lives and the cold
And everything hurt goes round and round and round.

Sunken Cities
(for Lynne Williamson)

Some wrecks the fish steer clear of and no
Life at all will inhabit them; others
Are cheerful tenements. Since you told me
Of dolphins living in sunken cities

On any blue clear day I imagine them
Arriving here and circling the spires
Slowly like eagles and down the standing
Canyons going faster than bicycles.

For rubble will not do. We must sink entire
Like Ladybower under the reservoir
Or under the two oceans that collide
Around the Wolf and under our ships'

Black shadows Lyonesse. After snow
When the white dome and Saint Mary the Virgin
Look frail on the sky and the gardens
Are blank and silent and sometimes

At evening when the great libraries
Light up like lanterns we are fittest perhaps
For the seabed and to open our doors
And windows to the incoming dolphins.

Landscape with friends

It was like hands when they extend
To greet us or offer fruit in a bowl
Or release a dove. The sun unclasped
And we admired the mountain in a new light.

It was the hour of the very long shadows
Pointing nowhere across the big fields
When the cypresses tap the darkness under the earth.
The fleece of forest on the mountain bloomed.

The gesture of the sun was almost sorrowful
Over the heads of our joy, as though
We missed the point. I praise the light,
I praise the mountain too that had

A self to show, but mostly I praise you
Little enough in the empty field against
That sea-green hill who stood your ground
Embracing and showing me your lighted faces.

At Kirtlington Quarry
(for Simon)

Catch, cricketer. Another year or so
Before you love the fit of a lampshell
Its promontory and pedicle hole
Quite the way I do

Or a section of the honey golden bed
Where the molluscs are lying as thick as leaves
Puts you in mind of Jews in chamber graves
Horribly impacted.

On the old floor, innocent and loveless,
Shapes were shapes, the lampshells swayed
Like nothing but themselves. We made
All the analogies.

Two hundred million years above us
The shape comes, ahead of its roar;
Seems too heavy to float on the surface air;
Has amazing slowness.

Lampshells shining in the oolitic snow;
Stars above all. The guards took bars to prise
The families apart. Here comes the noise
And shadow over you.

Tea-time

Tea-time. Instead of the tea-lady
Enter Aquarius. Fish, she says,
Marry me quickly. Backs the door to.
He sits like Piffy on the window-sill

Knowing she can see behind him, head-high,
Her river with its chunks of ice, stiff sheep
And the homes of fussy coots
Turned upside down. Do it, she says.

Handling the tiller of the tall window
He lets in the din and smell of the black melt.
In her bright eyes he is riding high in the stern
Of a ship of fools. Then the books lift,

The strict papers and the tight-arsed files
They flutter, they butterfly,
They snow up the room like doves, beating it to
The slitted window. Yes, she says, oh yes.

He has an ear for discipline. He hears
The lift land Mrs W.   Girl, he says,
Hold that door handle tighter than Katy did.
Oh come, she says, we shall be gone, she says.

NOTES

Piffy: a creature of indeterminate character and sex.
Mrs W.: the tea-lady.
Katy: the brave Scots girl, Kate Barlass, who bolted
the door with her arm to save her king.

Burning

I.

Brick tholos, heat
Humming about it in a strong sun.

She served in the dough
By a long handle. Bread
On the air, we lay
Idly in the camomile.

II.

Thatch, it burned;
The doors puffed open, the panes
Shattered like that woman's spectacles
On the Odessa Steps.
Bread had gone into the oven.
It burned.

Tashes of ferns for the pigs' bedding,
Hay for the cattle
Burned. The gorse in flames,
The broom ravelled to nothing;
The heather crackled.

What a squeaking of shrews.

III.

At low tide we entered a sea-cave.
There it was cold, fireless.
On the sea, as in an old perspective,
We saw charred little boats.

When the sea came home
We backed into the gullet,
Admired the vehemence of past tides
That had so rammed things in.
We remembered a picnic above:

How the sea thumped the air
And the ground blew cheerfully.

He felt for us.
Above the boulder choke
There was a small breathing space.

IV.

Our land is bumpy with tumuli.
The fire uncovered them.
Looters came
With bars and rooted at a blocked entrance
Or stove in the crown.
They will have found
Poor skeletons
No gold
A little earthenware.

V.

The fire blew into the sea.
The black earth raised innumerable foxgloves
Where in living memory there had been none.

We used to think the willowherb came in with the bombs
There followed such a flowering on the sites.

VI.

Into the dunce's cap
Inserting your little finger
Which is the little-bird-told-me
The listening finger
Inserting Baby Small
Under that snuffer
Wish, child,
Wish hard.

'We visit the house'

We visit the house: two blackened gable-ends
Their bedroom fallen in. They had perfected
The gift of lying still and sharing breath
Under one roof their tongues necking in silence,

He in her, fled to a small bud, inside,
Under her thatch, her lintel-bone, her capstone,
Shut-eyed, hibernated, and neither knowing
Exactly where it was, in whom, in what,

A new springwater was divined and roots
Struck quietly. Had they lain apart
They would have heard the low clouds tearing and
The fleeing constellations crying out.

Mother and Daughter

Mother and daughter were found standing
Unharmed in the bloody arena
On stage in the stepped hoofprint
Packed in mud. They had survived

A long bombardment of hot stones
And days of ash. They were found by feelers
Put out choking from a new well-shaft
Sunk for a villa riding high

Among sweet fields. Gently, gently
Resurrected they were thought to be vestals
But no, for certain, they are the mother and
Persephone still dumb from kissing Death.

Nobody loved the earth better than Demeter did
Who trailed it miserably
Calling after her child and nobody's gifts
Withheld were more pined after.

Mother and daughter passed north
From prince to prince and latterly
Survived the fire in Dresden. How Pompeii
Seen from the air resembles sites of ours:

Roofless, crusty. Look where Persephone
Wound in rags
Leads blinded Demeter by the hand
Seeking an entrance to preferable Hades.

The quick and the dead at Pompeii

I cannot stop thinking about the dead at Pompeii.
It was in the Nagasaki and Hiroshima month.
They did not know they were living under a volcano.
Their augurers watched a desperate flight of birds
And wondered about it in the ensuing silence.

There was sixty feet of ash over Pompeii.
It was seventeen centuries before they found the place.
Nobody woke when the sun began again,
Nobody danced. The dead had left their shapes.
The mud was honeycombed with the deserted forms of people.

Fiorelli recovered them by a method the ancients
Invented for statuary. When he cast their bodies
And cracked the crust of mud they were born again
Exactly as they had died. Many were struck
Recumbent, tripped, wincing away, the clothing

Rolled up their backs. They were interrupted:
A visiting woman was compromised for ever,
A beggar hugs his sack, two prisoners are in chains.
Everyone died as they were. A leprous man and wife
Are lying quietly with their children between them.

The works of art at Pompeii were a different matter.
Their statues rose out of mephitic holes bright-eyed.
The fresco people had continued courting and feasting
And playing mythological parts: they had the hues
Of Hermione when Leontes is forgiven.

Fogou

We are watching the sky in a certain quarter
For the look of iron. The house we leave
May be hospitable with the smell of baking bread
When we enter the ground again at the ferny hole.

What pity we shall extend into the sunlight
For our molested rooms, and what rank fear
That men will come prospecting with crowbars
Or slip in dogs at the mouth of our shorn hill.

The cold or fire; or to be sat out
By hunger; or as at Trehowlek
Where there were grave finds: a doll,
A photograph, the family loving cup.

At Pendeen something unspeakable
Must have happened to the woman of the house.
She appears in winter in a white dress
Biting a red rose.

Christmas

If his snowy manoeuvres
His chimneyings
Always seemed feasible
Why should not the big ship

After the seven seas
Sail our curdled river
Our stunk canal
And the unlit alley alley-o?

When the sky shrieked
And shapes were nosing through the water
And our big hospital
That could have blazed like a liner

Tried to hide, the galleon
Flew in like an owl
All sails breathing
Hoarsely like a baby

Behind the blackout
Hove to in our front room
And put off towards you
A coracle of oranges.

Hyacinths

The tortoise earth seems to have stopped dead.
Certainly the trees are dead, their limbs
Are broken, we can hear them clattering.
It must be about the midpoint. Last year
At this time you knelt for the hyacinths.

You brought them in like bread, in fired bowls,
From secret ovens of darkness. Three or four rooms
Soon had a column and a birth. Pictures show
The crib shining similarly
When Christ flowered from Mary the bulb.

The Kings stand warming their hands on the light.
Their gifts are nothing by comparison.
I suppose they feared that without some miracle,
Without the light and the bread of hyacinths,
The earth would never nudge forward out of the dark.

Mappa Mundi

1

This was a pleasant place.
This was a green hill outside the city.
Who would believe it now? Unthink
The blood if you can, the pocks and scabs,
The tendrils of wire. Imagine an apple tree
Where that thing stands embedded.

2

There is nowhere on earth now but
Some spoke will find us out
Some feeler from the impaled hill. On sunny days
That broken thing at the dead centre
Its freezing shadow comes round. At nights
Turning and turning like
The poor shepherd Cyclops for his bearings
It colours moonlight with a hurt eye.

3

Blood then, in a downpour.
For weather continued, the sun
Still drank what sea was available.
The indifferent wind herded his sagging clouds
That wept when they could not bear anymore.

4

Our nearest sea lies at the mercy of certain rivers.
The rivers themselves cannot avert themselves.
They begin blindly where, so we believe,
There is clean ice, snow and rare blue flowers.
They come on headlong and before they know it
We have them in our cities.

If they could die that would be better.
If they were lambs and we their abattoirs.
But they emerge like many of our children
Suddenly old, big-eyed,
Inclining to apathy. What was before
What they saw in our cities
They cannot at all remember. Day after day
They sink their trauma in the helpless sea.

5

The flat earth is felloed with death.
At every world's end, in some visited city,
Diminished steps go down into the river of death.
The salt river fills the throats of severed bridges.
Mors, the serpent, encircles the world.
His tail is in his mouth. He lives for ever.

6

Paradise lay in the river of death.
Before we slept we listened to the lapping water.
Our sands went steeply down, we bathed,
Rolling for joy like dolphins. Smiling,
We felt the dry salt on our faces;
Salt on our lips. She could halve
The mouth-watering apples exactly with her fingers.

We had four cardinal springs, they rose at the centre.
They rose from a love-knot continually undoing.

One day Charon arrived in a black boat,
One morning early, we were still sleeping.
Naked we were taken away from home.

7

The rivers of Paradise swam under the sea,
Unmixed with salt, death had no hold on them.
They surfaced miles apart, like fugitives
They calmed their breathing, they assumed
A local pace and appearance. Inland somewhere
Ordinary people
Receive driftwood from their broadcasting arms.

8

All rivers, even this, remain persuasive.
We have a house whose open windows listen.
At nights, my hand on your cold hand that rests
Upon your belly where our child curls,
We listen anxiously. Suppose we left,
Suppose we left this place and leaving below us
City, town, village and the interference
Of fence and throttling wire, suppose we found
The crack in the ice where one of the four emerges
Thrown, gasping, lying in the thin air
Like lambs that wait for strength from the sun to stand,
What could we do, holding that dangling thread?
Where could we go, knowing our need for breath?

Frightened at nights, hearing our city river,
We feel through our divining hands the pulse
Of the first four springs, we feel the kick
Of their departure diving, sweet through salt,
Their shouldering like smooth seals,
Their wriggling through the earth's rock like white hot quartz
Passing the creatures pressed
With starting eyes in carapaces
Whom fire and weight put out from the shape they had.

9

We shall not harm them now, they seem to pity us.
They have come out of a few last hiding-places.
They are solemn and curious, they have formed a ring.
Little by little they are coming forward, shy as birds.
We might have fed them. Or perhaps they are drawn
Against good manners, thinking it rude to stare, but as
Our children used to be drawn to pavement corpses
When deaths were singular. They are all true, all those
That we imagined; but many we never imagined.
They stare particularly at our little ones
Who cannot be frightened by anything we imagine,
Who are not alarmed by Blemyae and Sciapods,
By Dogheads, Cyclops, Elephant Men,
By some mouthless, feeding through a reed, others in a caul,
Some with the stumps of wings, some webbed, some joined, some
        swagged
With dewlaps, some diaphanous, some thin, with eyes.
Our children smile at them all. They are glad perhaps,
Our children, not to be unprecedented.

NEW POEMS

Local Historian

Come in for a reference he lay down,
The book on his chest, his finger trapped in its pages.
Slept, and the sea did what it always does
When we sleep and listen, the sea drew nearer
And the neighbourly black cypresses
Almost leaned over the house. Starlings
Drove like hail to the collection in the marshes.

Slept, out of hours, late winter in the afternoon,
His finger marking a reference, and with a whisper,
A shush, an exhalation, his library
Dissolved and a thousand saints and the local worthies,
Every carn and cross and cove, as fine as flour,
Sucked from the room like dust, like spores,
Name after name after name, the parishes,

All of Cornwall, slipped from his lease
Towards home. When he wakes, in the darkness
For a while he will not know where he is,
The sea making a din, the cypresses overwhelming.
But I know that man. His finger marking the place
He will go back to the lighted room where his writing is,
He will recall the truant parishes, once more.

A two-seater privy over a stream

All work, hitting at the buckled hills,
Stopped long ago. Trees have exploded
The dwelling house, but where they went and sat
Side by side for the resumption of innocence
Like pharaohs on two full moons
Their feet on a slate rest placidly
Their hands on their knees in the dry and out of the wind
(Except that the water shot through
Under their feet and moons and on the cold water
A colder draught was riding)
That place still stands. Well-built,
Homer would have called it, well-roofed.
The smooth wood is wormy but will support you.
I went in to eat an apple out of the rain.
Their bony hands. So high above Trawsfynydd
They had nobody upstream after the Romans left,
Always new water (after a rain
Like boiling quartz) and downstream not their worry.

The Pitman's Garden
(for Bill and Diane Williamson)

Man called Teddy had a garden in
The ruins of Mary Magdalen
By Baxter's Scrap. Grew leeks. What leeks need is
Plenty of shite and sunshine. Sunshine's His
Who gave His only begotten Son to give
Or not but shite is up to us who live
On bread and meat and veg and every day
While Baxter fished along the motorway
For write-offs Teddy arrived with bags of it
From home, which knackered him, the pit
Having blacked his lungs. But Baxter towed in wrecks
On their hind-legs with dolls and busted specs
And things down backs of seats still in and pressed
Them into oxo cubes and Teddy addressed
His ranks of strapping lads and begged them grow
Bonnier and bonnier. Before the show
For fear of slashers he made his bed up there
Above the pubs, coughing on the night air,
Like the Good Shepherd Teddy lay
Under the stars, hearing the motorway,
Hearing perhaps the concentrated lives
Of family cars in Baxter's iron hives.
Heard Baxter's dog howl like a coyote
And sang to his leeks 'Nearer my God to Thee'.
He lays his bearded beauties out. Nothing
On him is so firm and white, but he can bring
These for a common broth and eat his portion.

Leaving town, heading for the Ml,
Watch out for the pitman's little garden in
The ruined fold of Mary Magdalen.

The Vicar's Firework Show

Because he wanted St Paul's, full,
And a singing of praises to raise the roof
And got Duxford with Penton Mewsey
And a bare quorum to observe his puffs of breath

He thanks God for gunpowder. All Souls,
The tongues of his flock of dead ignite again
And whisper visibly. He climbs the hill outside
To pull a multitude, like Wesley

Packed to the mouth with speech, he draws a town
Of people roaring into the dark
And does what it is his call of work to do:
He gets them to look up: at the lifted word

Spilled on the sky. When that night
He offers the finished work of his hands
His year of peaceably fiddling with saltpetre
And all his secret inventions go up from the ground

With a thump and arriving rapidly
Out of a pinpoint open and hold
Wide open falling their pent-up souls
And the people respond with numerous similes

They call to one another what it is like
And repeat the brilliant insights of their children
So multiplying his illuminations
And a congregation of innocents is looking up

Earth seems an enviable place, a small
Warmth in the universe, and God's
Face feels for it like a blind man's. I name
That vicar the hope of those who join

And their hearts still hunger. I wish him
Snow for Christmas, deep snow, a hush
Over everything, a cessation, whiteness,
The town dumbfounded, and one sprig of flame.

A calvary on the Somme

It stays: a thicket of clenched fists,
A pack still menacing him with hands like maces or mines;
And beggars even as love fails
And a black hole is sucking him away

Still showing him what was done to them by diseases
Or by the law. It lasts on his retina
And here, inflicted: trees like guitarists
After the Civil Guard had wrecked their hands.

A skylark opens. One dead poet writes
Of shells that they sprinkled out of the sky like mimosa.
He wished his girl's breasts might be reddened at the nipples
Beautifully by the blood of him raining.

Every year the ground breaks out in an eczema of iron,
Lead and the bones of men and the poor horses
And somebody comes here with his instruments,
A gardener. The field raises its colours

On slag and larksong falls in generous handfuls.
Inborn in hands is the love of opening,
They love to race into leaf. A fresh forest
Soon assuages the head of Christ the medusa.

'He arrived, towing a crowd'

He arrived, towing a crowd, and slept
That night at the house of Simon
The leper, in Bethany, three miles out.
We know the rest. But Simon adds
A leper is good company for
A christ, each in his skin
So lonely and viewing the ordinary loves and trades
From a star through frozen lashes
(Simon whose face
Shines in a certain light like mother-of-pearl
Or a silver-fish). And when he blew
On lepers and pushed them gently
Back into the camp this only whitened him
The more. He was the cold
Blood-brother of Lazarus anointed by
A whore out of alabaster. His feet
Felt heavy in her net of hair
Like twins
Like bastards drowned.

The Saint observed at his Vigil

It was a strange sight.
He entered the North Sea like a candle
Long and upright, a pale man,
He entered and made two pauses:
Waist-deep, to suspend the animation of his parts
Chest-deep, to stun his heart.
I was afraid he would go under utterly
But at the chin he halted
And I saw his head alone on the sharp sea
And heard him yodelling across to God
His head under the whistling mobiles of the stars
His shining head
And the incandescence
I believe this was the soul of the saint
Climbed higher and higher in her drowning house.

Lord

Girls put up their bottoms in the lily-pond;
Thomas, an old defective,
Stood in the shrubbery with his breeches down
To wank at the visitors; but for the cave

His Lordship was at first undecided between
An anchorite and a Polyphemus;
Plumped for the former then: two hundred a year
And all found (water, crusts,

Cilice, hour-glass, the Good Book),
The appointment for seven years in the first instance,
The incumbent never to cut his nails or hair,
Accept gratuities, wander beyond the fence

Or speak. Upwind, taking tea,
His Lordship easily imagined the benefits of stillness –
The soul at home in the house of a quiet man –
And just as easily distress –

The man gone looking for his lost soul
In a labyrinth. At night
He watched for the rush of succubi
Bent on the candle of the anchorite.

There is a painting: His Lordship stands
Indicating the subject with a silver cane:
All hair, red feet and hands,
The mouth, oddly enough, wide open.

After the septennium he was renewed
As Polyphemus, required to eat mutton
And sing of the beauty of milkwhite Galatea
In verses of His Lordship's composition.

Anchorite

Dreaming yet again the bad dream
When he awoke there was a deep snow
And he decided to sin, sin hard
Against the snow that had fallen quietly while he sweated.

He cleared a space as wide as a lord's bed,
A green floor, the sky was blue again
When he began to shape her on that bed
Out of the gift of snow, the substance of heaven.

He made her after his lust: with open palms,
Blank eyes, the ghost of a smile, and raised
Her knees so he would fit. He marvelled then
That his unaccustomed hands had known his mind so well.

When she was made in the little verdant arena
Scooped out of the snow under the Mary blue
He did the thing that he was never allowed to do
In every dream. From a spotless eminence

The lord of the place observed him. Soon afterwards
The green sky wore the steady evening star
And the blade of the moon and where he had melted her
She froze, his face was glued to her face with his tears,

His arms were splinted on hers, his heart knocked
Faintly to be admitted. Then all the stars
Thickened the length of his back until he shone
Like something scaly that was shivering to death.

Man on his holidays

A man my age at Morecambe when the tide
Went out he went out after it with a little spade
And built a nude in the sand, her feet
Towards the sea. He did her open-eyed

Flat on her back or sleeping with her arms
Her pillow. He would be hours out there
Patting her with the spade and then with his hands
To get her curves right and the difficult hair.

Nobody came. At a distance, it is true,
There were some others with their trousers hoisted up
And hankies on their domes looking for scallop shells
And one playing noughts and crosses and one poor chap

In tears at a prospect of the Lake District
Across the bay. But when my friend had done
He sat back in his folding chair and waited for the sea
Which always came: it seemed the horizon

Unrolled, it came in rapidly, little low
Nibbling waves, and he watched his work: her feet,
Her thighs, her breasts, the careful likeness of her face
Blur and collapse under the sea's cool sheet.

Returning then he says he always felt
An old terror: of being so far out,
The sea teasing his ankles, the shore beyond his strength
And nobody adult who would hear him shout.

Came hurrying in with his little spade and chair,
Pressing his hand on a sharp stitch in his ribs,
And asked what he'd been doing out there that long
When he could speak he told the usual fibs.

Icarus

April 12 he entered as Pecker,
The indecent butler of her dreams, in tails
And bib (only) and balancing her tea
And biscuits chin-high. Guess what, he said:

They were building an Icarus.
That row like sports or quarrelsome fornication
Earlier and earlier above your visible sleep,
They were building a giant hope.

I woke on the crisp lawn, as though my father
Had sent me to watch for his twirling brush
And I saw the head of Icarus
Push through our roof with the determination of rhubarb.

A white face, a ghastly crown.
He wore a wreath of nests and little skeletons.
He shed a slithering cape of tiles
As he worked for the freedom of his plastered sails

And a sort of blood came into his face
When they brought him to bear on the egg-red sun
Though he looked as heavy as a battered windmill
He lifted. Now the whistling light

Enters through the star he made
And all the builders have gone. When I saw him
Impatience with gravity sprang in me,
Hatred of ceilings. Bounce, she said.

Mandeville remembered

In spring I wheeled him through the garden
Crushing the cockle shells, the paths
Enraged me, their perpetual
Digressions and dead ends, I couldn't think

My thoughts, letting him coast,
But must manoeuvre and shove hard and turn about
Seeing his dappled hands
Addressing an audience, and worse
His crown in its blather of white hair
Like the world egg
Lumped in chaos, the monologue
I swear was in the old coot's head
Like beaks, tapping for egress, he was cracked
And a swarm of dickybirds
In there was ready for the off.

Mandeville

He saw the agave flower and knew
A woman who had watched the phoenix burning
But for the once in a blue moon flooding of the Labyrinth
He found no witnesses and yet
It was the story he told best: how when
It happened the creatures congregated
To play in the turbulence as though this were
The bursting well that lies at the heart of Paradise
And swimmers passed, dreaming hand in hand,
Over the corridors of the Labyrinth
And viewed them from a height
Like Icarus. He evoked
The coming up of water
Out of the deep ear: the sob,
The chuckle, water's cleverness,
Her delight in rapidly solving intricacies,
He remembered this. I asked
Where was the Minotaur when the waters rose?
He answered: the Minotaur slept
The heavy head succumbed on his folded arms
Like a beaten boy, he wept, wept,
He dreamed himself a bubbling source of joy.

The Scaffolders

I.

These are my days of lead. I stare across
At Mandeville's great library where he beached
With all his souvenirs. Last week I watched
The scaffolders against the aqueous glass

Labouring upwards on the other side
In silence like the things without a shape
In depths of sea, in terrible depths of sleep,
Arrested things, aborted, efforts at flight

Sunk and encumbered, and although I pitied them
(Still beating) how could I wish them air
At last and the light knowing that what they were
Would always flounder and be burdensome?

II.

The gales lifted the leads. Raising my eyes
For once (a screaming of swifts) to the library's
Long and spacious roof I saw a man
Ascended there and strolling with a younger man

Against the sky, so shapely, so exact
Their living lines, and leading him to inspect
The drop on either side, and into every wind
He stood him, pointing. We are so far inland

But on high windows, after a southerly,
Like frost, I've heard it said, there'll often be
A lick of salt. The pointing man embraced
The boy around the shoulders, bare to the waist.

III.

They have come this side. I raise the heavy window
And watch them spit on their hands and begin the escalade
With a racket of iron and singing. I see now
That rising to where they will bask and promenade

142

Is nothing to them, thin cheerful men
Stripped for the sun, a bone charm at the throat
And a shining spanner on the thigh. When they have given
The uprights a sure footing they repeat

A pattern of bracing slants, they plank the walkways,
Lash in ladders sharp and rig at the head
For the roofers a handy crane so that with ease
Against gravity the parcels of new lead

May be called up and the traveller's fruitful ark
Be weatherproofed. Every last bolt
Is tight through its clasp. The scaffolders embark
On a quick and patient work, and leave it built.

Clare leaves High Beach
(for Steve and Sheila)

Others also were muttering and went
Each alone on the designated ways
Tipping their headgear. Said Doctor Allen,
His kind keeper, for such men
The best company in the world is trees.

Turmoil in the head, tempest: a beech
With its arms ripped off, the yellow bone
Showing, rags everywhere, the shriek
Of roots in air, and the mind reached
Into the crippling. He bolted then, for home.

Lay down, beat, his head the needle
North for the morning, he lay between
His two wives quietly and the love was equalled.
Woke. They were gone. The sadness welled
Out of the ground and through his eyes again.

A face came over him, it had a crown
That bulged from a wreath of hair, a face
As large and a dome as bald as the moon
Beamed down at him. It was his own:
Good-natured, cheerful, and quite crazed.

He lay for the north. Out of him travelled,
As though he bled, the love of certain trees
In place, a spire, a stile, a golden field,
Lapwing in thousands. How much he held
And must crawl after now on hands and knees!

'Under that bag of soot'

Under that bag of soot, when I moved it,
Something had been trying to grow. The light,
They think, as soon as the earth warms. Eyelessly
Start pushing. Then to be flattened and on the belly
Have to go feeling for help… Sunlight,

The gift of singing comes back to the birds,
And the things that had been doing their best to grow
Get up, they are white, they are a damaged yellow.
Nobody will ask such things to flower, only
To turn a decent green. A man like that

Released into the community with a shaved head
And the marks of fangs on his temples stands
Every day at the lights and when the green man shows
And everybody hurries he stands still, through red
And the next green he stands there like

Caspar on the asphalt with his wounded feet
And one little scrap of speech: that what
He wanted was to be a rider, but
He could smell the dead still growing in the soil
And the green he needed made him vomit.

The gardener of all this raises a merciful spade.

144

'There used to be forests'

There used to be forests beyond the peripherals.
We knew whenever one burned: it quietened our wheels
With skins and beheaded beasts would appear
Upended on the market and into the centre

There was a fall-out of the bipeds it evicted,
You saw them in the queues; or in the precinct, stupid;
Or getting the shittiest deals under the bridges;
And I used to think of Pan, naked, uprooted,

Limping on his goat-feet, come into town
After Daphnis died, and I tried hard to imagine
This town on a grief like that. Midsummer again.
Last night I woke from a dream crying my heart out.

Lovers forget the news. They will ask for places
Heard of near the perimeter and put
A pretty shock through the network but
Where will they run to when you catch their faces

Like souls in your blaring lamps, their clothes
Already fallen away and root and stem
Already they are being translated and from their mouths
The need for a forest babbles, bewildering them

Like antlers, the need for glades and pools, and as
Beasts they arrive where a whistling forest was
And clothing again is impossible and the moon beams
Back at the ash its last programme of screams?

The Forest

Pity about the forest gone up in smoke
And what comes out of it will surely die.
Not just the meat, also the funny folk:
The sow, the goat with faces haunted by
Humanity, the cross-betweens we give
A quid to goggle at, they never live.

Was on the tube once years ago in June
Late, on the wrong line, sleeping, very tight.
Opened an eye at let's say Bethnal Green
And slept again, thinking this can't be right,
And somewhere later, let's say Leytonstone,
Opened the other and a man got on

Naked as Adam, with a donkey's head,
And sat twiddling his ticket. Woke again
Somewhere, I don't know where, the place was dead,
I heard that wind come down the tunnels, then
Girl's steps running and the girl who ran
Got in and sat beside the donkey-man.

They filled my eyes, and when I heard the din
Of our wheels enlarge and we hit fresh air
And were into fields, outside, and blossom blew in
And touched his limbs, her dress, their heads of hair,
I felt we were a well of happiness
Struck luckily and coming up to bless

Mankind. They stood to leave, he steadied her
Against the fall, I saw how bare he was
Below the nape and how the head he bore
Flowered from a spine like mine, how courteous
And solemn his attentions were and what
A pride he showed, handing her down. I sat

Like some forgotten dosser in a pew,
The doors wide open, scents, a hubbub or
Music, a river noise – I knew
It was the forest they were heading for.
My ticket was wrong. I let the damned train start
Back for the city, back to its knotted heart.

Miranda on the Tube

An empty carriage – or nearly, there was a girl –
We all piled in, bigger than usual,
And sprawled or hung and the first strange thing
Was how we had kept our distance and left her space,
And then it stopped. I ask you: nowadays
Who stares like that? No man who wants his face
Leaving alone and certainly never a girl

Who's normal, but we flick our eyes at a face
And off again before the owner comes
Or stare a girl to the floor, but there between
Stations halted, a nightmare for a girl,
She stared at us, at every one of us
In turn and all together and the strangest thing
Was this: she thought us beautiful, it showed

Like an open flower, it shone, it seemed her eyes
Were hands already learning over us
The human, the phenomenal, incredulous.
O faces soft as roses! We reviewed
Our boots, the worst came up in everyone
Like puke, out of the heart, our mouths were full
Of reason upon reason why we should not be

Looked at as though we were beautiful by her
A total stranger halted nowhere near
Help and wanting none. A carriage comes
Empty almost never and a girl alone
Never who looks like that. I sometimes see
A face a bit like hers: it hangs between
The smashed-up stations, sad as a bag-lady's.

A blind elephant man in the underground

He is still under the park where I saw the girl
Sunning her face. Her eyes were closed and such
A blessing she gave mine, smiling to herself,
I wished it down through the roots to cure London.

Travellers nearer the surface may send up
A tremor into our feet but where he is
Is where the nearly sheer escalators end
And haul themselves out of it. People gave him

The wall and a thoroughfare along
Their cold shoulders and he came through untouched
Like Moses, sweeping with his stick, and his
Right hand was open to avert us. But if

No girl like the one in the upper air
Has let his fingers model another face
On hers and practise smiling on her smile
Then he has no comparison in his head

During his lifetime in the multiplying
Corridors under London when he rides
The worm and alights in the small hours somewhere
Deserted and draws his head into shelter.

Jailed for Life

In where I put her she had always said
There was a frightening thing but I put her there
And slept on it, to teach her. Morning after
I went down with my candle. First our steps
Then it was different: a weapon in my hand
And I was knocking against wet walls and louder
And louder there was a roaring noise, it stank
Like in a cage and I was going down on paths

Calling her littlest name in like a shell
Or lug, hearing a roaring, seeing the stumps
Of legless men and smelling an animal.

Then out. There was a beach and she, my kid,
Was leading the thing she had been frightened of
By the hand and it was blind and its great head
Was hurting it in the light, an arm like Samson's
Thrust out, and ballock-naked, the poor thing
With its bull's head, and she was leading him
With daisies in her hair to a little boat,
Some men of the island bowing.
                       Stood there
With my daft candle in the sunshine, gripping
Our coal hammer and watched her sail away.
The men put on their caps and looked right through me.

Quay

The launch is late, we wait on the hot quay.
Our farewell conversations are giving out.
That little shark from yesterday
How white it looks, how sad its mouth;

A team of crabs is operating on it.
Crabs are the stupidest among the living down there.
Netted with shrimps they never mind the net
But crunch like fun. You can haul them anywhere

On anything edible. Stag's littlest daughter
Is gouging a limpet out. End of the season,
They will be gone home soon. With his father,
The Drowner, mothers used to shush their children

And some still do, with him: his one eye,
His black appearance. Hunched in his tractor
He is thinking he will kiss that holiday woman goodbye
If she looks his way once more.

His girls have landed a crab on the hot concrete.
It sidles and fences, bubbles at a vent;
Black in the sun. They squeal for their bare feet.
Its scratchy legs pick at our nerve-ends.

The launch rounds the point like sudden death.
Clatter of starters, the tractors edge down.
We shall leave, we shall be over and done with.
Stag's girls are screaming, that crab has gone to ground

The last place it should: under his wheels
And he is on hands and knees searching the shadows
With his head's one eye and his hand crawls
Under the racket of the engine after the claws.

His shirt rucks up, we see his white backbone
And are glad when he surfaces, though the black lid
Over his eye has slipped. His hand has won.
He fits the crab snugly under the tractor's tread.

Oh, we have time enough to interfere
And look a fool. The crab merely waits
Folded between the concrete quay and the tyre
And nobody moves. We wait. I see its

Eye. Then Stag backs over the carapace.
His girls giggle. The woman, in tears,
Comes through the mêlée from her rightful place
And bruises his mouth with hers.

The Island of Curieuse

I wake. She wakes. I weep.
She knows I am weeping for the Island of Curieuse
So clear to me: the rain
Like nothing we witness here
Coming with the lightning
In sheets the blue of Hell
And the storm-wind when I wake
Continues for several minutes in broad daylight
The surf rakes everything to itself
The sea wins
The killing sea takes all.

Lilith

I think of her more when it is cold.
Snow-light: waking very early
I saw nothing in the garden that was alive
But puffy birds. Last night my son,
At the telescope, called me into his freezing room.
Threads of the light of his eyes, minuscule darts,
Had traversed an infinite cold distance
And struck into a moon.
He was bent over the slide, making a commentary,
But I was looking down the white garden
To the fence and the one lombardy poplar
And could see nothing that was alive.

'I should not be dreaming of you like this'

I should not be dreaming of you like this.
There was a staircase, we were not surprised
After the fountains and the tumbled statues
To begin a marble stairs. You ran ahead
Lifting your sodden dress, and I should have known
By your laughter which was not like the laughter
Of a real girl out of breath but like
The merriment of water it was a race
And I was trailing. Where the stairs gave out
Where they were broken off you waited for me.
I saw you backed against finality
Quite still, your open hands were by your sides
And you were showing me your pointed breasts
And smudge of hair and smiling at my grief.
We were so high above the ruined garden
I was afraid and you were not afraid.
You took my fingertips, I felt they were cold,
And blew on them and weighed them in your hands.
I knew that you were turning me to stone
And all the buoyant blood was in your veins.
Then cracks ran through the marble from my feet.
You stood me on the lip. Now fly, you said.

'In the ocean room'

In the ocean room, in the history of voyaging,
The best he showed me was the giant nautilus.
We were cheek by cheek, pressing against the glass,
When one or other of us began imagining
Sleep underwater and the old way of breathing.

He was the pearly nautilus and I
Allowed my body to the way he rocked.
So we tolled forward and with my fingertips
I read the scrimshaw: poems, fables, the log
Of landfalls, idle beautiful lines

As long as thong but flowering queerly
And becoming another creation. Couched on him
I read and silvery tickling bubbles
Hurried from my mouth. In the next case
There was a photograph of a savage man

All mapped out, he wore the fabulous
Whole world, not an inch of him was free,
And he wore it under the skin that rubs away.
His wife (I read) with the point of her tongue
And nails at night had inked and coloured him in.

Swimmer and Plum Tree

The clod was between his legs, the thin trunk prone
Across his thigh. I came and went,
I could only watch so long, but all afternoon

He sat on the dug ground in the sun, content
With his knife in the roots. He said it was ditched
And they had brought it home. The roots were pent

In a net, impacted, desperately stitched
In and out of the mesh through every single square
As fine as centipedes, embedded, clutched.

Not looking up, he said he remembered my hair
When I was swimming, water through all the strands,
Such a fine combing, and did I not wish I were

Unravelled out of him? I watched his hands
Feel gently with the knife, his fingers tease,
Loosen, release. The swimmer's hair extends

Her down the river, as though the sea's
Moon-ridden body sucked on her she slips
Easily into water. I sometimes raise

The swimmer I was – the river parting from her lips,
She holds steady with strokes, her head
Wearing the river like a bride – and then she dips

And drowns. The bole was upright in his fist. He said:
Now it can breathe again. He showed it me,
Its shock of gladdened roots. I am afraid

Soon he will write that the frail arms of their tree
Have blossomed while I am clenched and the small cone
Of the soul under my hair is weighing like mercury.

'I am inconsolable'

I am inconsolable because of her laughter.
You must have put something into her mouth
That flowered and overflowed like the living water
Between her lips she had flowers coming out

And dribbling down her neck and throat and all
The length of her like Madalena's hair
When she sat up it was a waterfall
Of laughter and nothing else that covered her.

You must have put something under her tongue.
I heard it entering her blood like power
And I lay dumbly where I don't belong
Like somebody else outside your open door

Thirsting to death and given nothing but laughter –
Hers – to drink and wishing I could swap
My tongue for hers and clog her mouth up where
The laughter was coming from and make it stop.

Emblem

Here is a woman holding an orange tree.
She must be waiting to change houses
And by the way she holds it in her lap
She will not part with the little orange tree.

I suppose the time of year to be winter
But the orange tree holds the three living seasons
(Leaf, flower and fruit) in the woman's hands
In earth, in an earthen pot, in her lap.

Bare boards, windows bereft of curtains,
Gaps on the walls where there were pictures:
But she is sitting quietly on a broken chair
In her warm coat, holding the orange tree.

DAVIES

A NOVEL

Davies was famous for a moment in 1911 when Home Secretary Winston Churchill raised his case in the House of Commons. But who was Davies? In this fictionalised account of a lifelong petty criminal, David Constantine unravels the mystery of a shadowy loner caught in a vicious circle of self-perpetuating crime.

David Davies (1849-1929) was known in his day as the 'Dartmoor Shepherd'. He spent half a century in prison for a succession of minor offences, mostly for stealing coppers from the poor boxes of local churches.

Davies came from Llanfyllin, Montgomeryshire, and Constantine has set his novel in the counties of the Welsh Marches. He has made much use of documentary material – Hansard, newspaper reports and a biography – and aims in his novel to seek a truth behind established facts. Although historically based, *Davies* is a novel whose concerns are very much relevant to the present day, particularly in its portrayal of the habitual offender and of vagrancy.

'*Davies* is a remarkable achievement, and not least for its bitter frugality of style...Constantine pieces Davies together from mist and myth, godly persecution and tolerance...The result is absorbing and disturbing' – CHRISTOPHER WORDSWORTH, *Guardian*

'The poet David Constantine speaks up for the socially edged-out ...In *Davies*, Constantine's spare bare-knuckle prose makes marvellously present the harsh existence of his hero'
– VALENTINE CUNNINGHAM, *Observer*

'Constantine's unabashed seriousness has marked him out as a very European writer – an impression confirmed by his first novel *Davies*, which, with its documentary neutrality of tone and muted outrage at injustice, recalls, for example, the Böll of *The Lost Honour of Katharina Blum* much more than any contemporary British novelist's work' – TIM DOOLEY, *Times Literary Supplement*

Hardback: ISBN 0 906427 91 6   £7.95

Friedrich Hölderlin
SELECTED POEMS
TRANSLATED BY DAVID CONSTANTINE

Friedrich Hölderlin (1770-1843) was one of Europe's greatest poets. The strange and beautiful language of his late poems is recreated in English by David Constantine in these remarkable verse translations.

'Hölderlin is a poet we can read with our atrocious times in mind. He is a deeply religious poet whose fundamental tenet is absence and the threat of meaninglessness. He confronted hopelessness as few writers have, he was what Rilke called 'exposed'; but there is no poetry like his for the constant engendering of hope, for the expression, in the body and breath of poems, of the best and most passionate aspirations' – DAVID CONSTANTINE

'Hölderlin's tragic life has become, in Keats's phrase, 'intrinsically figurative'. We too easily see him as an archetype: the marginalised visionary in an age of mercantile philistinism. The poems, on the other hand, are more elusive. Their religious intensity and their classical framework, their density and their verse forms all run outside the major English traditions. His poetic world is one of fracture, absence and loss. The long central poem 'The Archipelago' offers a terrible vision of the human condition. Set against this darkness, however, is the brilliance of the ideal, which for Hölderlin found its most absolute manifestation in Ancient Greece. The memory of this perfection is at once our salvation and our grief, for it reminds us of our loss and yet engenders a longing for future renewal...

'Along with lucid, informative notes, the selection contains an excellent biographical introduction. There the reader is pointed towards Michael Hamburger's monumental translation of Hölderlin's work...Constantine allows himself more freedom and goes for an 'equivalence of spirit' in a more familiar idiom. This is at once a bold and a humble undertaking, and has produced poetry of a remarkable luminosity and intensity, written in rhythms and cadences which recreate, both in their extremities of grief and their urgent hope, the immediacy of the original' – KAREN LEEDER, *Oxford Poetry*

Paperback: ISBN 1 85224 064 4   £5.95

David Constantine was born in 1944 in Salford, Lancashire. He read Modern Languages at Wadham College, Oxford, and from 1969 to 1981 was a lecturer in German at Durham University. He is now Fellow in German at the Queen's College, Oxford. He is married with two children, and lives in Oxford.

His first book of poems, *A Brightness to Cast Shadows* (Bloodaxe Books, 1980), was widely acclaimed. His second collection, *Watching for Dolphins* (Bloodaxe Books, 1983), won the 1984 Alice Hunt Bartlett Prize, and his academic study, *Early Greek Travellers and the Hellenic Ideal* (Cambridge University Press, 1984), won the first Runciman Prize in 1985. His first novel, *Davies*, was published by Bloodaxe in 1985. His third collection, *Madder* (Bloodaxe Books, 1987), a Poetry Book Society Recommendation, won the Southern Arts Literature Prize. His *Selected Poems* (Bloodaxe Books, 1991) is also a Poetry Book Society Recommendation.

His other books include a critical introduction to the poetry of Friedrich Hölderlin (Oxford University Press, 1988), and a translation of Hölderlin's *Selected Poems* (Bloodaxe Books, 1990). His translation (with Helen Constantine) of *Spaced, Displaced* by Henri Michaux is a launch book in the Bloodaxe Contemporary French Poets series (1992).